CHILD OBSERVATION SKILLS

PHILLIP T. SLEE

CROOM HELM
London • New York • Sydney

© 1987 Phillip T. Slee
Croom Helm Ltd, Provident House, Burrell Row,
Beckenham, Kent, BR3 1AT
Croom Helm Australia, 44-50 Waterloo Road,
North Ryde, 2113, New South Wales

Published in the USA by
Croom Helm
in association with Methuen, Inc.
29 West 35th Street,
New York, NY 10001

British Library Cataloguing in Publication Data

Slee, Phillip T.
    Child observation skills.
    1. Child psychology — Methodology
    I. Title
    155.4'18   BF722
    ISBN 0-7099-5408-5

Library of Congress Cataloging-in-Publication Data

Slee, Phillip T.
    Child observation skills.

    "Published in the USA by Croom Helm in association
with Methuen, Inc." — T.p. verso.
    Bibliography: p.
    1. Child psychology — Research — Methodology.
2. Observation (Psychology) I. Title.
BF722.S58   1987   155.4'072   87-15549
ISBN 0-7099-5408-5

Printed and bound in Great Britain by
Biddles Ltd, Guildford and King's Lynn

CONTENTS

FIGURES AND TABLES

Figures

Tables

FOREWORD

Observation is a skill and it is acknowledged that direct observation skills are both an art and a science. Certainly, the ability to utilize observation skills is a unique asset. Without them, the practitioner would be ineffectual and the researcher would lose invaluable data. These skills however, are not the kind of talent with which clinicians or researchers are automatically endowed nor are they the sort of talent that is generally acquired through academic training.

Unfortunately, however, there has been a lack of attention given to the manner in which individuals, particularly children, can be observed as a way of acquiring additional clinical data. Traditionally, experience over time seems to provide the main way whereby observation skills are refined and enhanced. Rather than rely on specific instruction or courses, professionals and researchers alike have had to depend on their own personal intuitions and experiences as a means of observing clients.

Observation skills however, are now coming into their own right. This book, for example, reflects that shift in emphasis and represents a major endeavour to document the nature of observation from its theoretical foundations right through to applied practice. In part, this move in research methodology away from quantitative data to more qualitative information heralds the need for a book of this type. Simply, although some clinicians and researchers are wanting to move away from the more traditional means of acquiring information, they do not have the knowledge nor resources with which to elicit that additional data.

Observational skills of the sort described in this book are also applicable across a range of mental health, education, medical, and applied settings. These skills are not distinctive to one professional treatment orientation or field setting. There is a sense then, in which they are multi-disciplinary and can be shared across professions in a way that is conducive to effective work environments.

Indeed, there is little doubt that child observation skills are critical, but unfortunately, information on how to adequately assess children through observation techniques has been lacking. This book is a step to rectify that omission.

Daryl G. Cross, Ph.D.
Superintendent
Child and Family Centre,
Adelaide Children's Hospital

DEDICATION

This book is lovingly dedicated to my mother who showed me what it means to have faith and courage in the face of adversity and to my father who allowed me the freedom to be.

PREFACE

The idea of writing this book developed slowly and looking back on why I finally committed myself to print I am inclined to reflect that "it seemed like a good idea at the time". In setting pen to paper I was confronted with challenging, frustrating and important conceptual and practical issues at every stage of the writing. This book in no way represents an adequate resolution of the issues but rather a commitment on my behalf to at least address them. Consideration of these issues reflects the ongoing development of my own ideas about the nature of child observation.

At its conception, the orientation of the book was very practical. In the course of writing though, it quickly became apparent that the practical orientation was bounded by an identifiable, if implicit, body of theory. Every effort was then made to explicate the theory upon which the practice of child observation could be based. This outlook reflects my current belief that the selection or advocacy of a methodology is profoundly theoretical.

What started out then as a "how to" book, developed into an examination of the issues that I would regard as central to the field of child observation. The science of child observation currently stands at the threshold of new and exciting developments. The directions such developments take will depend on what one means by science. In this book it is argued that to date, a rather narrow conception of science has constrained the development of child observation. The whole question of the nature of science and what passes for knowledge is presently undergoing critical examination in the social sciences. The way is now open for developing new methods of child study.

PHILLIP T. SLEE

ACKNOWLEDGEMENTS

Special thanks to all who contributed to the book, especially Kieran Wallace, Sarah Lawson and Katie Lawson. The photography of Paul Wallace and skilled art work of Timothy Slee are particularly appreciated. Special thanks to my loving wife, Elizabeth, for all her support. I would also like to thank in order of appearance Dr. Allan Russell, Dr. Michael Lawson, Dr. Neil Piller, Dr. Ken Rigby, Mr. Peter Battye, Mr. Ken Hancock and Dr. Darryl Cross for their time, effort and constructive criticism in reviewing the manuscript. Grateful thanks are also extended to Ms. Joy Grossman for her careful work and ever present cheerfulness during the typing of the book.

Chapter One

SEEING CHILDREN

I have no name: Pretty joy
I am but two days old   Sweet joy but two
What shall I call   days old,
    thee?   Sweet joy I call thee
"I happy am   Thou dost smile,
Joy is my name"   I sing the while
Sweet joy befall thee!   Sweet joy befall thee!

(W. Blake, 1971)

INTRODUCTION

A quick look through the relevant sections in the local library or bookstore will show that through the ages children have been the subject of description at the hands of poets, novelists, philosophers and playwrights. However, the development of systematic methods for the study of children is a relatively recent phenomenon. Dietrich Tiedemann is acknowledged by historians of child psychology as a pioneer in the field of systematic research into child development. Tiedemann published a study of his own child in 1787 predicting that his own observations would be followed by many others. True to his prediction, the late nineteenth century witnessed a growing interest in child observation studies. Presently, even a cursory glance at the literature in developmental psychology indicates a blossoming of the field in the last half century. Today, courses in child observation embrace a range of professions including teaching, psychology, social-work, child-care, and nursing, to name but a few.

WHY STUDY CHILDREN?

The motivations for studying children are as broad

1

and complex as the field itself. In part it is recognised that through the study of children's behaviour we may come to better understand adult behaviour. As John Milton noted in *Paradise Lost,* "The childhood shows the man, as morning shows the day."

From a somewhat different perspective Charles Darwin believed that the child was the link between animal and human species. As such, by observing the development of the infant some understanding could be reached of the species itself. Many of Darwin's observations were based on studies of his own children. For example, Darwin argued that emotional expressivity was basically a physiological matter and that expressive gestures were largely universal and innate. "Everyone who has had much to do with young children must have seen how naturally they take to biting when in passion. It seems instinctive in them as in young crocodiles, who snap their little jaws as soon as they emerge from the egg" (Darwin, 1965, p.241).

Other investigators were less interested in comparing human and animal species than Darwin. Thus, the Frenchman, Gabriel Compayre (1896) believed that information concerning the child's early years would serve to illuminate later development. "If childhood is the cradle of humanity, the study of childhood is the cradle and necessary introduction to all future psychology" (Compayre, 1896, p.3).

More recently, Medinnus (1976) identified four main reasons for studying children including:
1. an intellectual curiosity concerning natural phenomena
2. the need to gain information to guide children's behaviour
3. increasing our ability to predict behaviour
4. the need to understand our own behaviour.

People working with children are now more than ever aware of the need for the study of children. Thus, for teachers, the study of children is a critical component in the development of instructional programs, management of children in the classroom and in enhancing teaching effectiveness. For psychologists and family therapists, understanding children's behaviour facilitates the counselling process and the development of therapeutic programs for children and families. Social workers make extensive use of research involving children in their daily dealings with families. However, while there exists a growing recognition of the importance and need for the study of children, systematic methods for child study are still undergoing considerable development and refinement.

Before addressing the issue of methodology though, important consideration needs to be given to the broad philosophical question of how it is that we come to perceive and know the world around us. In turn, this question will provide a deeper understanding of how it is that we "see" children and it is from this perspective that the field of child study and problematic issues concerning the methodology of direct observation are best viewed.

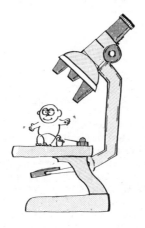

SEEING IS NOT NECESSARILY BELIEVING!
In his exciting and refreshingly honest book, A Guide for the Perplexed, E.F. Schumacher (1977) addresses the key question of how it is that we perceive and understand the world of which we are part. It is a question that has occupied the time and thought of philosophers and mystics down the ages.

> We live in a world of unreality and dreams. To give up our imaginary positions as the centre, to renounce it, not only intellectually, but in the imaginative part of our soul, that means to awaken to what is real and eternal, to see the true light and hear the true silence (Thoreau, 1960, p.12).

Schumacher argues that our five bodily senses render us "adequate" to understand the world at the lowest level of being but that all that is supplied by our sensory receptors is a mass of "sense-data". To interpret the sense-data, abilities or capabilities of a different order are required and Schumacher refers to these abilities as the "intellectual senses". "As regards the bodily senses, all healthy people possess a very similar endowment, but no-one could possibly overlook the fact that there are significant differences in the power and reach of people's minds" (Schumacher, 1977, p.51). At this point, an illustration of the vagaries of the observation process taken from Lawrence Blair's book Rhythms of Vision (1976, p.30) may be instructive.

When Magellan's expedition first landed at Tierra del Fuego, the Fuegans, who for centuries had been isolated with their canoe culture, were unable to see the ships which were anchored in the bay. They were so far beyond their experience that, despite their bulk, the horizon continued unbroken: the ships were invisible. This was learned on later expeditions to the area when the Fuegans described how, according to one account, the shaman had first brought to the villagers' attention that the strangers had arrived in something, something which although outside their experience could be seen if one looked carefully. We ask how could they not see the ships - they were so obvious, so "real" - yet others ask how we cannot see things just as obviously real.

To summarize then, it appears that "... different observers or the same observer at different times, may get different information from a picture" thus illustrating "how the observer 'projects' on to the picture i.e. contributes ideas or meanings of his own" (Abercrombie, 1969, p.44). As such, our responses to the environment are determined not only by the direct effect of external stimuli on our biological system but also by our past experience, our purposes, and the individual symbolic interpretation of our experience. As the French mystic Simmone Weil so sensitively expresses this sentiment: "The beauty of the world is not an attribute of matter itself. It is a relationship

of the world to our sensibility, the sensibility
which depends upon the structure of our body and
soul" (1973, p.119). Some brief consideration is
now given to the manner in which our relationship
to the world influences our perception of children.

SEEING CHILDREN IN CONTEXT

There are a number of illustrations that may be
drawn from art, literature and philosophy which
demonstrate how children have been perceived
differently by observers. Phillippe Aries (1962)
has argued that childhood as we know it today is a
relatively recent phenomenon. In medieval western
society, adults and children were seen and treated
in much the same way. For example, children of 3
years of age were expected to work at certain
cottage industries. The eighteenth century
novelist Emile Zola in his book Germinal depicts
12 year old children working alongside their
fathers, older brothers and sisters in the
coal-shafts of France.

In developing his theme, Aries argues that the
term "childhood" relates to differences in
knowledge and social behaviour between adults and
children. For example, in relatively complex
societies (western industrialized societies) such
differences are recognized within specific social
institutions, e.g., schools. That is, divisions
such as infancy, toddlerhood, early, middle and
late childhood and adolescence may be arbitrarily
created in relation to different levels of family
life and schooling. However, in less complex
societies children are simply treated as miniature
adults. Despite the recognized weaknesses of
Aries' arguments (e.g., the incompleteness of
historical records upon which his information is
based) it does appear that the way people viewed
children several centuries ago is markedly
different from the perception of children today.

Another illustration of the differing
perceptions of children across time is found in
the way artists depicted children. For example,
in medieval paintings of nativity scenes, the
infant Jesus was painted with quite adult-like
features. The Flemish artist, Peter Breughel
painted children as miniature adults. It is
highly unlikely that the artists were technically
incompetent and a more reasonable interpretation
is that they were reflecting the point that
children were not seen in the same way as they are

today. As children were not thought of in the same way as they are today, the artists did not see and paint them in the same way. As Poole (1972, p.6) notes, "The meaning attributed to what goes on in the significant space before our eyes will vary according to our moral presuppositions, the partial vision we receive, the position we occupy in the perspectival world."

Apart from the historical context, the prevailing philosophy of science also provides a filter through which we see children. Presently, the dominant western view of reality draws heavily upon a belief in a particular view of scientific method as the only valid approach to the acquisition and understanding of knowledge.

The basis for the prevailing scientific method is drawn from the world view of empiricism. The British philosopher John Locke (1632-1704) was the primary force in the development of empiricism, the philosophy of which did much to replace scholasticism (a philosophy embracing a world view of a god-ruled static cosmos) as the prevailing world view. Empiricism advocates that all knowledge is derived from experience. As Locke noted:

> Let us suppose the mind to be, as we say white paper, void of all characters, without any ideas; how comes it to be furnished? Whence comes it by that vast store, which the busy and boundless fancy of man has painted on it with an almost endless variety? Whence has all the materials of reason and knowledge? To this I answer in one word, from experience: in that all our knowledge is founded, and from that it ultimately derives itself (Locke, in Russell, 1974, p.589).

David Hume (1711-1776) further developed Locke's philosophy (Russell, 1974). He focussed specifically on sensation, advocating that research drawing directly on experience through the senses was the means by which knowledge of the world was acquired.

With empiricism as its basic building block, the nineteenth century witnessed the triumph of science over philosophy and religion as the means for gaining knowledge about the world. As conceived by Auguste Comte (1798-1857) science referred to the natural sciences such as biology, chemistry and physics (Russell, 1974). Comte believed that human behaviour, institutions and organisations could be investigated and studied by applying the methods and principles of the natural sciences. His philosophy came to be known as positivism.

As argued by Battye and Slee (1985), empiricism reflected in a positivist epistemology is now firmly entrenched as the prevailing world view or paradigm in the social sciences, including psychology. Underpinning this world view are four propositions regarding the nature of science which may be coupled under the rubric, the unity of science "thesis" and "scientism" (Evans, 1979). These propositions maintain that:

Scientism
1. science gives the whole truth about the nature of reality
2. science gives us the ultimate truth about the realities it deals with

Unity of Science Thesis
3. there is one method which all genuine sciences employ
4. this method consists of giving deterministic causal explanations which are empirically testable.

In its most basic form, positivism is concerned with establishing causes and with predicting events or behaviour. Humans are regarded as passive inert organisms whose behaviour is directed or caused by external forces. This simplistic cause-effect model of human behaviour draws very heavily on how most people think physics is done. Unfortunately, as noted by Heather (1976, p.19) "...it is a supreme irony that modern physics has long abandoned the mechanistic determinism of the last century which psychologists in their anxiety to be seen as respectable scientists continue to copy". The point being made here is that all scientific observation, experimentation and measurement occurs within a philosophical framework. The dominant framework at any time represents the basic canon of faith guiding the conduct of enquiry.

This description of the evolution of the prevailing positivist paradigm has been necessarily brief and incomplete, and for a more complete discussion of the issues touched upon here the interested reader is referred to Gauld and Shotter (1977) and Manicas and Secord (1983).

The ramifications of the view are however, considerable, and to understand this, some brief explanation of a world view or paradigm is necessary. In the broadest sense of the term a world view helps people interpret, understand and bring some order to their lives. Thomas Kuhn (1970) elaborated the notion of paradigms (from the Greek paradigm or pattern) and their role in the scientific endeavour.

In general terms a paradigm might be considered as essentially <u>how</u> we can meaningfully use terms like "knowledge", "information" and "science". It serves to identify the types of theories used in research, identifies the problems worthy of investigation and the methodology to be employed in investigating the problem. As Palermo (1971, p.136) noted in describing the nature of the paradigm:

> These conceptions are the rules for playing the game of science; they are formed more by common law procedures than by fiat. They determine the way in which the world of the discipline is viewed, and make it difficult for alternative conceptions to be considered.

In relation to disciplines such as psychology and education, the dominant influence of a positivist paradigm has emphasised the "senses" as the factual basis for understanding human behaviour. A literary embodiment of this attitude is found in Charles Dickens' novel <u>Hard Times</u>. The demand for facts comes from one of the characters who tells the teacher "Now what I want is Facts. Teach these boys and girls nothing but Facts" (Dickens, 1968, p.11). As Manicas and Secord (1983, p.99) note, "Psychology has become far more sophisticated in its methodologies and procedures and has generated a large body of knowledge ... but the philosophy of science that is implicit in contemporary psychology has not changed all that much".

One unfortunate aspect of the pre-eminence of the positivist paradigm in the social sciences has been a polarisation of the debate about alternative ways of knowing and understanding the world around us. All too often the debate has been simplified into the dichotomies of "quantitative vs qualitative", "hard vs soft", "rigour vs intuition" and so forth. In simplifying the discussion to this extent, the overriding implication we are left with is the incorrect notion that there is one "good" or "correct" method for doing science. The notion that will be taken up and developed in this book is that a growing number of writers and researchers are coming to question the "unity of science" thesis amid a growing recognition that something more than "sense data" is required to better understand human behaviour (e.g., Harré & Secord, 1972; Gauld & Shotter, 1977; Reason & Rowan, 1981; Manicas & Secord, 1983).

Observers of children, for example, whether parents, teachers or psychologists, adopt a theoretical framework which guides or filters their conception of child development, methods of study and frequently the instrumentation used in research. More often than not, the theoretical framework is not recognised or explicitly stated. For example, in her book, Delamont (1984) levelled severe criticism at a decade of classroom research in the United States of America with its emphasis on the description of overt behaviour, the categorisation of behaviour and the focus on small bits of behaviour rather than more global facets of classroom interaction. Such research, in reflecting the dominant positivist paradigm, presents a particular view of children's and teachers' behaviour in the classroom. It disregards the description of aspects of behaviour not directly amenable to the senses such as the value, intention or meaning inherent in human behaviour.

CHAPTER SUMMARY
As described in this section, the task of "seeing" children is a deceptively simple one. Historical, cultural and philosophical considerations mediate and influence our perception of children and their behaviour. In this book particular consideration is given to the relationship between the prevailing philosophy of science and the direct observational study of children. Care is taken to identify how the prevailing positivist philosophy of science prescribes how direct observation research should be conducted including how and where the observations should be made, methods used to collect the data and the means for interpreting the information collected. More particularly, consideration is given to an increasing acceptance by researchers that no one

methodology can answer all the questions we have about children and their behaviour. Alternative outlooks on the nature of the observational process are outlined.

OVERVIEW OF THE BOOK

The field of child study has a short history but a long past. Children and their behaviour have provided a focus of interest down the ages. However, the development of techniques for observational research are still in the formative stages. Typically, the bulk of currently available texts on child observation seems to fall into a number of categories. There is the "cook book" text, where its practical orientation is used as a justification for making minimal reference to the underpinning theory or paradigm upon which the book is based. Then, there is the text which will acknowledge that there are different ways of looking at, or studying the world, but which fails to seriously address the issue of how the ways differ. For the most part, books falling into these two categories largely reflect, albeit implicitly, the current dominant positivist paradigm concerning the nature of science and how science should be conducted. Finally, there is the text which carefully outlines the different ways of knowing and investigating the world, but which fails to provide guidelines for conducting such research. In the present book, every effort is made to identify as clearly as possible, the implications of adopting a particular paradigm for the way observations are conducted, the data recorded and analysed and the results interpreted. An important related feature of this book concerns the linking of theory with practice.

In the present text, the stance adopted is to link philosophical issues with questions of research practice as closely as possible. The argument is that the selection of a particular methodology is profoundly theoretical. Research methods represent different means for understanding the phenomena under study. To choose one method over another is to foreclose on the possibilities for understanding a phenomenon from alternative perspectives. Moreover, it is argued in this book that the methods one chooses stem from beliefs and values we hold about the nature of reality.

PLAN OF THE BOOK

In the present book a number of issues relevant to the broad and complex field of child study are addressed. In Chapter 2, consideration is given to ethical issues in the study of children. In Chapter 3, various research designs used in observational research are described. Chapters 4 and 5 are concerned with describing various methods for recording behaviour along with practical exercises illustrating their use. The focus of Chapter 6 is upon strategies for recording behaviour, including checklists, voice recorders, event recorders and video-recorders. In Chapter 7, guidelines are provided for researchers interested in developing their own coding scheme for direct observation. Chapter 8 is oriented more to the clinical application of child study methods. For example, the role of direct observation in the classroom and in assessing parent-child interaction is examined. Chapter 9 draws together different facets of the observational process identified in the text and outlines a model for describing the nature of observational research.

> When the voices of children are heard on the green
> And laughing is heard on the hill,
> My heart is at rest within my breast,
> And everything else is still (W. Blake, 1971).

Chapter Two

ETHICAL ISSUES IN CHILD STUDY

> In unequal relations it is right, since
> everybody should be loved in proportion to his
> worth, that the inferior should love the
> superior more than the superior loves the
> inferior: wives, children, subjects should
> have more love for husbands, parents, and
> monarchs than the latter have for them
> (Aristotle, in Russell, 1974, p.187).

INTRODUCTION

Before setting about the task of observing or
studying children careful consideration is needed
of their rights and the ethics involved in
research. As elaborated in the following
discussion there is an urgent need for such
consideration in the face of the growing interest
in child study. More generally the issue of
children's rights and ethics of research are
important in terms of the overall struggle for the
recognition of the dignity of all human beings
regardless of age, race, sex or colour.

Concern for, and interest in, the rights of
children, is a relatively recent phenomenon. The
topical subject of children's rights reflects a
burgeoning interest in child development research. In a closely related way it also reflects
changes in our understanding of the nature of
childhood. As childhood has emerged as a legitimate
subject of study in its own right some awareness
has emerged of children's vulnerability and the
responsibility of adults for children's economic,
social and psychological health. It is an
indictment of contemporary western society that in
the present book a chapter is needed on children's
rights. The necessity of the chapter reflects
vestiges of the outlook expressed by Aristotle
(noted above) that particular members of western

12

society, e.g., children, are still considered
unequal in worth and hence undeserving of
equivalent love and consideration.

CHILDREN'S STATUS IN SOCIETY

Any study of children's status in society must be
grounded in historical context. History shows
that for centuries children have been looked upon
as property and more particularly as the property
of their fathers. As Oxenberry (1976, p.10) notes
"Paternalistic care has been the hall-mark of the
parent-child relationship". Right up to the
present time children have lacked the means to
redress wrongs against them. The state has been
reluctant to become involved or interfere in
family relationships.

Some basis for understanding the contemporary
status of children in western society is obtained
from the writings of Aristotle. In Bertrand
Russell's description of Aristotelian ethics it is
noted that, while Aristotle considered human
beings as ethically equal, "the justice of a
master or a father is a different thing from that
of a citizen, for a son or slave is property, and
there can be no injustice to one's own property"
(Russell, 1974, p.186). The basis for viewing
children in terms of proprietary interest has a
long history.

English Law elaborated between 1300 and 1800
A.D. prescribed the relationship between parent
and child in terms of trust. The parent's rights
emanated from the Crown and the Crown reserved the
right to intervene and protect the child's rights
and interests. However, as Fraser (1976, p.322)
notes "while the court would intervene to protect
a child's interests, it did not provide the child
with a vehicle to present his grievances to the
court, nor did it guarantee the child the right of
independent representation."

Apart from the law, some interesting insight
is gained into the status of children in western
society from the writings of seventeenth and
eighteenth century philosophers such as Thomas
Hobbes, John Locke and John Stuart Mill. Hobbes,
writing in the seventeenth century, argued that
children were cared for solely because they were
capable of serving their fathers, and should be
assigned a position of complete dependence. "Like
the imbecile, the crazed and the beasts over ...
children ... there is no law". (Hobbes, 1931,

13

p.257). The implication of Hobbes' argument is that children have no natural rights and no rights by social contract because they lack the ability to make formal contracts with other members of society and to understand the consequences of such contracts.

Later in the same century John Locke, arguing from a somewhat different perspective, considered children as under jurisdiction of their parents until they were capable of fending for themselves. Until such time children were considered to lack understanding and therefore could not assert their will. Unlike Hobbes, Locke believed that both adults and children possessed certain natural rights which needed protection. Parental benevolence was believed to be sufficient to ensure that children's rights were protected. Locke's outlook rejected the proprietary aspect of parenthood in place of making children God's property. In describing children as lacking in understanding, Locke reflects the view that children need to develop adult capacities for reasoning and understanding. Until such time parents are under a God given obligation to care for children. By implication, where parents fail to fulfil their obligation to children the state may be empowered to do so.

The nineteenth century witnessed a rising concern for the excesses of child labour and the industrial revolution. Childhood, with its special needs, came to be recognised as a distinct stage in human development. More recently, the field of developmental psychology has contributed to the recognition of divisions in the concept of childhood itself. Over and beyond infancy, at least three stages of child development are broadly identifiable including early childhood, middle childhood and adolescence. Psychology has served to emphasise the different needs of children at the various stages in their development. However, its contribution to the current debate concerning children's rights has been almost negligible. In reviewing the literature, it appears that the process of recognising children's rights has been impeded by an historical legacy. This legacy incorporates the view that in western society children were accorded few rights even of a derivative kind. These rights have accumulated over the centuries. The marked reluctance of society to recognise the rights of children reflects a fear that to do so would threaten the preservation and stability of the family unit. Other writers are quite pessimistic about the rights of children in contemporary western society. Moreover, increased understanding and concern has not been coupled with increased rights. As a consequence, children's rights have actually diminished for we have simply replaced ignorant domination with sophisticated domination. With increased attention to children has come resentment. Our efforts to shape children, to reform them, to fix them, to correct them, to discipline them, to educate them, have led to an obsession with the physical, moral and sexual problems of children; but they have not led to our liking them more, or realising their potential (Farson, 1974, p.66).

CHAPTER SUMMARY
Historically it is possible to identify a number of shifts in emphasis in the status of children in western society. Certainly, the proprietary aspect of childrearing is well grounded in history. As Oxenberry (1976) notes through all this, the child has been seen as a natural part of the family unit. A child is conceived by his parents, belongs to them, inherits what is theirs and is subject to their rearing. The historical context makes it quite clear that a child is owned, in a chattel-like fashion, by the parents. Some modification to this outlook has occurred with the emergence of the caretaking conception of child protection. However, despite the contribution of psychology to our understanding of the physical, social and emotional development of children, far more work is required in the way of identifying children's rights in our society.

THE RIGHTS OF THE CHILD
In 1959 the United Nations issued the Declaration of the Rights of the Child. In summary, the declaration states that every child should have the right to affection, love and understanding, to adequate nutrition and medical care, to free education, to full opportunity for play and recreation, to a name and nationality, to special care of the handicapped, to be among the first to receive aid in time of disaster, to learn to be a

15

useful member of society and to develop individual abilities, to be brought up in a spirit of peace and universal brotherhood and finally to enjoy these rights regardless of race, colour, sex, religion, national or social origin.

More recently, in 1979 an International Colloquium in School Psychology drafted a Declaration of the Psychological Rights of the Child. In brief, the Declaration notes that the child has:

1. The right to love and freedom from fear
2. The right to personal, spiritual and social development
3. The right to education and play.

Of course, if charters such as these are to have any force, the people who study and work with children must be aware they exist, understand the principles espoused and be prepared to act as advocates and put policy into practice. Active involvement at this level is required to prevent the declarations becoming empty rhetoric lacking the force required to bring about real change in the status and rights of children in our society.

CHILDREN AND RESEARCH

In psychology generally there is a growing awareness of the ethical issues involved in therapy and research (Brown & Slee, 1987). But declarations such as those just described assume particular importance in relation to the psychological study of children. The proliferation of research in various fields such as teaching, social work and psychology has not been accompanied by a similar growth in understanding and legislation regarding the rights of children involved in such research. For the most part the generally accepted attitude involves a caretaking conception in as much as the researcher is believed to have the child's best interests at heart. One is entitled to be a little sceptical of such an attitude given that adults do not always fully understand children's needs or interests.

There currently exists the potential for real conflict between children's rights and the requirements of research. For example,

- students in the teaching and health-care professions are frequently required to observe and study children as part of course requirements.

- researchers in various child related professions are under increasing pressure to conduct research to advance in their profession.
- the outcome of research is increasingly used to determine policy and guide professionals in relation to the education and welfare of children.

All too often in pursuing ends such as these, the rights of the children participating in the research are overlooked or ignored. As such, the following guidelines serve a significant and timely reminder of the ethical obligations of researchers working with children.

Table 2.1. Ethical Standards for Developmental Psychologists

1. No matter how young the subject, he has rights that supersede the rights of the investigator of his behavior.
2. The investigator uses no research operations that may harm the child either physically or psychologically.
3. The informed consent of parents or of those legally designated to act in loco parentis is obtained, preferably in writing. Informed consent requires that the parent be given accurate information on the professional and institutional affiliation of the investigator, and on the purpose and operations of the research, albeit in layman's terms.
4. The investigator does not coerce a child into participating in a study. The child has the right to refuse and he, too, should be given the opportunity to refuse.
5. When the investigator is in doubt about possible harmful effects of his efforts or when he decides that the nature of his research requires deception, he submits his plan to an ad hoc group of his colleagues for review.
6. The child's identity is concealed in written and verbal reports of the results, as well as in informal discussions with students and colleagues.
7. The investigator does not assume the role of diagnostician or counselor in reporting his observations to parents or

those *in loco parentis*. He does not report test scores or information given by a child in confidence, although he recognizes a duty to report general findings to parents and others.

8. The investigator respects the ethical standards of those who act *in loco parentis* (e.g., teachers).

9. The same ethical standards apply to children who are control subjects, and to their parents, as to those who are experimental subjects. When the experimental treatment is believed to benefit the child, the investigator considers an alternative treatment for the control group instead of no treatment.

10. Payment in money, gifts, or services for the child's participation does not annul any of the above principles.

11. Teachers of developmental psychology present the ethical standards of conducting research on human beings to their students.

Statement of Division of Developmental Psychology of the American Psychological Association, *Newsletter*, 1968, pp.1-3.

Chapter Three

RESEARCH DESIGNS

> Research design is the plan, structure, and
> strategy of investigation conceived so as to
> obtain answers to research questions and to
> control variance (Kerlinger, 1973, p.300).

INTRODUCTION

Methods of child study have passed through a
number of phases in the last 50 years. During the
1930s and 1940s direct observation was very much
in vogue. For example, researchers such as
Goodenough (1931) and Dawe (1934) used direct
observation in their study of the development of
emotional expression in children. Emphasis then
shifted from observation to interview and
questionnaire procedures during the 1950s. The
assumption underlying this methodological shift
was that children's behaviour could be best
understood by analysing parental beliefs and
attitudes.

The late 1960s and early 1970s witnessed a
renewal of interest in the use of observation
procedures in child studies. Research was
typically laboratory based in nature. To this
end, writers such as Bronfenbrenner (1977) and
Hartup (1979) drew attention to the limitations
that laboratory studies placed on understanding
human behaviour and called for observational
research with wider ecological validity.
Currently, emphasis is being given to the study of
children in more naturalistic settings such as the
home (Lytton, 1980; Russell, 1983; Slee, 1984).
As such, while direct observation has generally
been acknowledged as a cornerstone of the
sciences, its use in the social sciences has
suffered from fluctuating fortune. Presently
though, there is renewed interest in the use of
direct observation in child study (e.g., Lamb,

Suomi, Stephenson, 1979; Field, Goldberg, Stern, Sostek, 1980; Lytton, 1980).

In this chapter a brief description is given of research designs that may be used in observation. Broadly speaking, the research design might be considered as the plan formulated for collecting relevant information on the research problem. At the outset though, it is necessary to emphasise that the whole question of research design is more complex than can be treated in this single chapter. The interested reader is referred to relevant texts such as Kerlinger (1973) and Reason and Rowan (1981) for further information.

RESEARCH DESIGNS IN DIRECT OBSERVATION
In Table 3.1 a number of research designs for the observational study of behaviour are listed.

Table 3.1. Strategies in the Observational Study of Behaviour

---

Field Studies
Naturalistic Experiments
Field Experiments
Laboratory Studies
New Paradigm Studies

In choosing a design or combination of designs for observation research a number of questions need to be addressed. First, what is the paradigm from which the strategy is drawn? As noted in Chapter 1, paradigms are influential in shaping the theory used in guiding research, the problems worthy of investigation and the methods used in research. Secondly, what are the advantages and disadvantages of each design in relation to the problem under investigation? Thirdly, when might it be appropriate to use a particular design?

Field Studies
Kerlinger (1973, p.405) defines field studies as "ex post facto scientific enquiries aimed at discovering the relations and interactions among sociological, psychological and educational variables in real social structures". Ex post facto refers to "after the fact" investigations, that is, naturally occurring incidents. As such,

in field studies the researcher does not attempt
to deliberately manipulate the situation and every
attempt is made to minimize the observer's
intrusions on the observations.

Festinger and Katz (1953) identify two types
of field studies, namely, (i) exploratory, and
(ii) hypothesis testing. In the exploratory
study, investigators are concerned with
discovering significant variables identifying
relationships among variables and generating new
hypotheses. Field studies focus more on
describing than predicting behaviour.

In hypothesis testing, the purpose of the
investigation is to discover relationships among
variables. It is often erroneously believed that
observation of naturally occurring events
precludes the testing of hypotheses. However,
recent statistical advances, namely sequence
analysis, whereby one uses the occurrence of a
behaviour at one point to predict the likely
occurrence of the same or other behaviour at
another point, has facilitated hypotheses testing
in field studies. For example, Patterson (1979)
tested the hypothesis that parents' punishing
behaviour suppressed a child's hostile and
aggressive behaviour. Using sequential analysis
he found that parents' punishing behaviour did not
suppress children's hostile or aggressive acts.

Not surprisingly, advocates of field studies often challenge the nature of findings obtained in laboratory studies, arguing that the experimental method is an artificial one which does not allow the researcher to generalise findings beyond the experimental situation. Barker (1963) in arguing for field studies notes that "a science which does not include amongst its data phenomena as they exist unarranged by the investigator and without input from the methods used to reveal, describe and enumerate them is only half a science" (p.5).

In a later book, Barker (1968) suggests that data obtained from laboratory studies be called "operator data" as it is produced by means of special operations performed by the experimenter. That is, the experimenter in developing the experimental situation, deciding upon the task to investigate, how the subjects will perform, and what they are to respond to, is structuring the situation.

Advantages of field studies relate to the immediate and first-hand nature of the data. Furthermore, recent technological innovations such as video cameras have vastly improved data gathering and storage procedures. Advances in statistical procedures have also allowed researchers to make suggestive causal inferences about the nature of behaviour.

Disadvantages of field study designs relate to their ex post facto nature. As such, it is difficult to control all the variables that might be contributing to a behaviour. For example, think of all the variables that might contribute to a child's behavioural problems in the classroom, e.g., family background, personality and intellectual functioning, to name but three.

For the most part, field studies are recommended for use in the exploratory hypothesis generating stage of research. This view largely reflects the positivist influence in psychology with its heavy emphasis on reducing a complex whole into component manipulatible discrete entities and with isolating causal explanatory factors. Presently though, there is an increasing interest in the use of field studies in developmental psychology fostered by a growing concern that "much of contemporary developmental psychology is the science of the strange behaviour of children in strange situations with strange adults for the briefest possible period of time" (Bronfenbrenner, 1977, p.513).

Research Designs

Bronfenbrenner (1977) further noted that a survey of child development research indicated that some 76% of research was of an experimental-laboratory nature, contrasting with 8% which used naturalistic observation designs. Presently then there is a very real need for field studies in child development.

Naturalistic Experiments

In a natural experiment the researcher uses opportunities that spontaneously arise to study behaviour, where that behaviour is changed by natural circumstances. For example, Zucker, Manosevitz and Lanyon (1968) assessed the effects of anxiety and social interaction patterns during a power failure in New York City. MacFarlane and Raphael (1984) examined the effects of bushfires in South Eastern Australia upon victims' behaviour.

Not surprisingly, the obvious disadvantage of having to wait for natural experiments to occur limit the extent to which this research design is used in child observation studies. The advantage of the research design is that it allows for greater opportunity than natural field studies to isolate causal factors.

Research Designs

Field Experiments

In distinguishing between a field experiment and a field study it is necessary to understand that the difference lies in the control the researcher has over the independent variable or the event(s) being studied. A field experiment involves the deliberate manipulation of an independent variable in a naturalistic setting. For example, Parke, Berkowitz, Leyens, West and Sebastian (1977) investigated the impact of exposure to violent and non-violent films on the social behaviour of adolescent boys. The films were shown where the boys lived and the amount and type of aggression shown by the boys in relation to the films was assessed in the same area.

The field experiment overcomes the disadvantage of the natural experiment in having to wait for an event to occur. It offers the researcher the important advantage of having control over the variables likely to influence the outcome of the experiment, thus facilitating the identification of causal factors. Of course, the control of variables in field experiments is still not as tight as in laboratory studies. Field experiments also provide an opportunity to study complex social influences and behaviour in realistic settings and can be used in the investigation of a wide range of problems.

Disadvantages of the field experiment design stem largely from practical considerations such as time and cost and ethical issues. Ethical problems arise from assigning individuals to experimental and control groups where benefits may accrue from being in one or other of the groups. For example, in testing a new reading program on children in the classroom one group may be discriminated for or against by the experimental intervention.

Laboratory Studies

As already noted, Bronfenbrenner (1977) found the bulk of child development research to be of experimental-laboratory design. Foremost among the factors contributing to the dominant influence of this design in research is the current philosophy of science. As noted in Chapter 1, the prevailing model or paradigm influencing the western view of reality draws heavily upon a belief in the scientific method as the only valid approach to the acquisition and understanding of knowledge.

24

Research Designs

The scientific method is the means by which scientists set about testing theories. In turn, theories about behaviour give rise to predictions or hypotheses which can be tested in controlled settings. Controlled laboratory settings offer the experimenter the greatest possible opportunity for holding constant all the extraneous variables that might be influencing behaviour.

Using the positivist conception of the scientific method, the most effective means for testing a prediction is to deliberately manipulate the independent variables and then observe the changes in the dependent variable. This method aims at revealing cause and effect relationships. For example, the effect of television violence on children's behaviour might be tested by showing groups of children violent and non-violent television programmes (independent variable) and then observing children's behaviour toward each other (dependent variable). The experimenter might choose to control for extraneous factors likely to influence children's reactions to the television programmes by matching children on variables such as age, sex and socio-economic background. Further details on the nature of laboratory designs are available in texts such as Kerlinger (1973). Briefly though, advocates of the scientific method argue that it provides for the natural identification of causes of behaviour and allows for greater precision and replicability than other research designs.

Criticisms of laboratory designs come from various sources. Koan and McGuire (1973) argue that such research is not designed to test carefully formulated hypotheses but to demonstrate the investigator's abilities as a stage manager. "What the experimenter tests is not whether the hypotheses are true but rather whether the experimenter is a sufficiently ingenious stage manager to produce in the laboratory conditions which demonstrate that an obviously true hypothesis is correct" (Koan & McGuire, 1973, p.449).

More serious criticisms of laboratory experiments relate to what critics have identified as fallacies in the positivist paradigm upon which the design is based. As such the first problem arises from the sheer complexity of human behaviour. In laboratory studies, the experimenter attempts to reduce behaviour to its basic elements in the search for causation. As Heather (1976, p.32) notes, "The fallacy here is to believe that the complexity of human psychology can be reduced in this way or, conversely, that adding up these simple results will ever amount to a picture of what human life is really like". A related problem which then arises concerns the extent to which results obtained in the laboratory can ever be extended to "real-life" situations. Another criticism of laboratory studies concerns the tendency for subjects to develop their own understanding of the purpose of the experiment and to behave accordingly.

In summary then, a review of the literature will show that research designs based on laboratory studies are extensively used in child development research. In choosing to use such a design in observational research it is imperative that one is fully aware of the philosophy of science underlying the design and the associated advantages and disadvantages of the approach.

New Paradigm Research Design
As noted in Chapter 1, the philosophy of science influences or filters the way we view children. More particularly, as noted in this chapter it also influences the way we do science. The

observational research designs described to date in this chapter are all firmly rooted within the positivist empirical tradition. Outside the mainstream empirical tradition there exist other very important, but widely neglected methods for designing studies involving children. In this section brief consideration is given to a newly emergent "method" for conducting research which has been labelled as "new paradigm". To date, no agreed upon name really exists for the "new paradigm" method. In the literature it is variously referred to as "hermeneutics" (Harré & Secord, 1972) while Manicas and Secord (1983) speak of a "realist theory of science" and DeMaria (1981) employs the term "a priori research". Unlike the previously described research designs where philosophical underpinnings draw heavily upon positivist conceptions of science, new paradigm research has no clearly identifiable origins. Rather, the methods have been developed and adapted from various disciplines including anthropology, sociology, philosophy and psychology. As described by Reason and Rowan (1981), the basis of the new paradigm lies broadly within the purview of the behavioural sciences. Influences acknowledged from within psychology include the writings of humanists such as Maslow, Fromm, and Rogers and ideas from the personal construct theory of George Kelly. Further afield in sociology and anthropology consideration is given to the methods of phenomenology and participant observation.

Reason and Rowan (1981) have identified numerous ways in which new paradigm research differs from mainstream research and the interested reader is referred to their book for a more complete discussion of the differences. In reviewing the literature though, it is possible to identify two distinguishing features of the new paradigm research (Battye & Slee, 1985). These include (i) the view of people as reflexive agents and (ii) the questioning of science as a value-free pre-suppositionless endeavour.

An important feature of new paradigm research is the emphasis it gives to the view that people are reflexive agents. That is, people are seen as having the power to initiate change, make changes and act on decisions.

People act for certain purposes and goals and attach some freedom of choice to these acts citing reasons for their behaviour; reasons which are often guided by values. People take responsibility for their acts and it is reflexivity or the capacity for self reflection which is a characteristic feature of human action (Battye & Slee, 1985, p.24).

The view of people as reflexive agents is considerably different from mainstream psychology's conception of people as passive organisms largely shaped by forces in their environment.

Another feature of new paradigm research concerns the challenge it has issued to the notion that science is an objective, value-free enterprise carried out by neutral detached observers. As Capra (1982, p.77) notes,

The patterns scientists observe in nature are intimately connected with the patterns of their minds; with their concepts, thoughts, and values. Thus, the scientific results they obtain and the technological applications they investigate will be conditioned by their frame of mind.

Of course, scientists argue that the methods of science are specifically designed to minimize the impact of subjective bias. This is true, but a revolution is occurring in the philosophy of science concerning the notion that science is an objective endeavour. Facts are ordered within frameworks or paradigms. As such, while the detailed research of scientists will not explicitly depend on their value system, the larger paradigm within which research is pursued will never be value-free.

As already noted, the research designs employed in the new paradigm research are still in the process of development. In essence though, the researcher would accept as given, the complex scene encountered and take this totality as the data base. In addition to observation material, the researcher might interview the participants and have them complete questionnaires. The interview and questionnaire data is usually intended to identify subject's attitudes, values, beliefs and goals. Such information is considered critical in helping interpret or explain the observed behaviour. The researcher does not make such a strong distinction between observer and observed and is more likely to adopt a participatory role in the observation process. This approach contrasts sharply with the accepted scientific approach whereby the observer is instructed to be as unobtrusive as possible. In Chapter 5 further details are provided of particular methods involved in conducting new paradigm research.

Chapter Summary

The research design is the plan that is developed for testing a psychological prediction. In this chapter, consideration has been given to the advantages and disadvantages of various research designs. It has been argued that in choosing a particular design, careful thought needs to be given to the particular paradigm upon which the design is based.

Chapter Four

METHODS OF DIRECT OBSERVATION

What is this life if, full of care,
We have no time to stand and stare?

(W. Davies, 1944)

INTRODUCTION
The whole process of "watching and wondering" is
one that has occupied the attention of behavioural
scientists for a considerable time. From teachers
interested in better understanding children's
classroom behaviour, social workers trying to
understand a child's behaviour during therapy to
psychologists observing mother-infant interaction,
the concern has been to develop and refine methods
of observation. Although direct observation is an
appealing strategy to use investigators may soon
find themselves on uncertain ground. Questions
concerning the most appropriate observation method
to use must be addressed.

In this chapter a number of direct observation
methods and their advantages and disadvantages are
described. Practical exercises are provided to
illustrate the methods. The methods described
include:
1. Baby biographies
2. Anecdotal records
3. Specimen descriptions
4. Event sampling
5. Time sampling
6. Rating scales.

The methods of child observation described in this
chapter have been developed and applied largely
within the purview of a positivist paradigm. As
such, the limitations of the various methods
presented in this chapter must be understood in
this context. In Chapter 5 where an alternative
strategy for collecting observational data is
described, more serious limitations of the

methods outlined in this chapter will become apparent.

BABY BIOGRAPHIES

One of the oldest forms of observation is the diary type account that parents keep of the behaviour of their children. The first published diary description of an infant was written by the German philosopher Dietrich Tiedemann (1787). Charles Darwin kept notes on his son Erasmus born in 1840. Darwin's observations were on the whole quite accurate although at times some crude generalisations or interpretations were drawn from a limited data base. For example, Darwin noted of Erasmus:

> When two years and three months old, he became adept at throwing books or sticks etc. at anyone who offended him; and so it was with my other sons. On the other hand, I could never see a trace of such aptitude in my infant daughters; and this makes me think that a tendency to throw objects is inherited by boys (in Kessen, 1965, p.121).

As a scientist father, Darwin was also interested in experimenting to further understand the nature of his children's development. Thus, he tried such things as touching the sole of the baby's foot or the side of his face to observe the reaction:

> During the first seven days various reflex actions, namely sneezing, hiccoughing, yawning, stretching and of course sucking and screaming were well performed by my infant. On the seventh day I touched the naked sole of his foot with a bit of paper, and he jerked it away, curling at the same time his toes, like a much older child when tickled (Darwin, 1965, p.100).

A more contemporary example of a baby biography is provided by the following diary type account a young mother has kept of her first baby's behaviour.

Methods of Direct Observation

Baby's name: Sarah

15 weeks: Notices fluffy toys suspended from bar over bouncer.

1 year: Retrieves book from bookshelf and slides it along floor until she finds an adult willing to read it to her.

14 months: Can throw a ball and place rubber rings on a stick; loves fluffy toys.

15 months: Loves to listen to Patsy Biscoe records. Plays with plasticine - draws with crayons.

17 months: Loves to draw - can hold a pen properly and draw fine lines on a page.

Advantages of Baby Biographies

1. An important advantage of the method is that it facilitates understanding of the development of behaviour over time. As Shinn (1900, p.11) notes, "the biographical method of child study has the inestimable advantage of showing the process of evolution going on, the actual unfolding of one stage out of another, and the steps by which the changes came about". Some insight into how a baby biography would illustrate a child's development over time is illustrated in the mother's description of Sarah provided earlier.

2. Another strength of the method is that it provides a full and rounded picture of various aspects of the child's behaviour encompassing as it usually does a good amount of detail. That is, it helps capture the complexity of the child's growth including physical, social, emotional and cognitive development.

3. Baby biographies can serve an important hypothesis generating function where numerous questions are raised about the child's development from the rich complexity of the descriptions.

Disadvantages of Baby Biographies

1. One disadvantage of the method concerns the generalisability of the findings. Typically diary type accounts are kept by

well educated, interested adults and as such the descriptions could not be said to be representative of the general population.

2. The method can also suffer from bias in observations. All too often the biases of the loving care-giver are apparent in the interpretation of the data.

3. Thirdly, there is often a failure to separate interpretation from observation.

4. The method is also quite time consuming requiring as it does extensive periods of observation.

Application of Baby Biographies to Child Study

Currently the method is used infrequently in child study. One aspect of its use though is to be found in case studies such as Virginia Axline's (1964) Dibs - in Search of Self or Clara Park's (1967) The Siege. In these books the authors utilize extensive diary type observations of children to help understand and explain the child's development.

In an interesting variation on the method, Massie (1980) used sets of home movies parents had made of their infants to examine the nature of parent-child interactions. The home movies were of children who subsequently developed one of the forms of early childhood psychosis, autism, symbiotic psychosis of childhood, childhood psychosis or childhood schizophrenia. Massie analysed mother-infant interaction in the home movies for timing (rhythm of interaction), the initiation, maintenance, termination of behaviour, spatial relationships, physical force and feeling or affect.

Guidelines for Using Baby Biographies

1. Ideally records should be kept on a daily basis.

2. The records should be as extensive as possible. It is better to record too much data than too little.

3. Every attempt should be made to sort out observation of behaviour
(e.g., infant moved its head from side to side) from interpretation (infant was angry).

4. The observations should be written up as soon as possible.

Methods of Direct Observation

PRACTICAL EXERCISE ONE: DIARY DESCRIPTION OF A SINGLE CHILD

Introduction
To become familiar with the concept of diary descriptions, it would be worthwhile reading a book such as Axline's Dibs - in Search of Self.

Procedure
Select as your subject a child whom you are able to observe regularly over a period of months. A sufficient length of time is required in order to obtain some insight into the changes and developments taking place. If only a short period of time is available, then a young infant is perhaps the best subject, given the rapid changes taking place in the social, cognitive and physical areas of development in the first year of life. Each day spend some time (preferably an hour or so) with the child. Keep note of the observations in a diary or exercise book. Record as much of the child's behaviour as you can during observation.

Date(s)	Ss	Age	Context of Observation
24.1.82	Sarah	6 months 1 day	Lounge room floor

Observation	Interpretation
The mother Dianne is in the kitchen baking biscuits for her brother. Sarah is playing with a fluffy toy bear while sitting on the floor. Sarah begins to vocalize "da-da-da"!	Sarah is content and happy playing by herself – engrossed in playing with her favourite toy.

Methods of Direct Observation

Questions to consider
1. To what extent did your observations capture the essence of the child's behaviour?
2. Were your observations specific and detailed or general in nature?
3. How easy was it to separate observation from interpretation?
4. How could the observations be improved upon?

ANECDOTAL OBSERVATIONS
Anecdotal records differ from baby biographies in as much as the investigator is less concerned with the behaviour of individual children and more concerned with recording behavioural and verbal responses in general. One of the earliest published accounts of the method is provided by Ellen Haskell (1896). In her book entitled Child Observations First Series, some 1208 anecdotes of children's imitative behaviour were presented.

Like diary descriptions, anecdotal records are often written in narrative style. It is not necessary to note every detail of the subject's behaviour though, because the focus is upon specific incidents, e.g., imitative behaviour, co-operative behaviour, altruistic acts, and so forth. The following example illustrates an observer's anecdotal record of a child's imitative behaviour.

Myles, a 4 year old boy is on a day's outing with his parents when they stop at a hotel for a drink. After seating themselves in the saloon bar mum says "I think I will have a whisky and dry". Dad says "I'll have a beer" and then asks Myles what he would like to drink. Myles looks carefully around the room at the various posters advertising drinks and after a considered pause says in all seriousness "I'll have a double whisky".

Advantages of the Method
1. It is a relatively easy method to use. That is, it requires no time frame, no special setting or environment and requires no special code of categories.

2. Anecdotes serve an hypothesis generating function making one think about child-

ren's behaviour. They stimulate further study of children's behaviour.

Disadvantages of the Method
1. It is a very time consuming method requiring that considerable time be spent in observation.
2. Considerable work is required in establishing the reliability and validity of the observations.

Guidelines for Recording Anecdotal Observations
Brandt (1972) has set out the following guidelines for the use of anecdotal observations.
1. Write down the anecdote as soon as it occurs.
2. Identify the basic actions of the key person and what is said.
3. Identify the setting, time of day and activities involved.
4. In describing the central character's actions also include the response of others in the situation.
5. Wherever possible use the exact words to preserve the flavour of the conversation.
6. Preserve the sequence of the episode; i.e., an anecdote has a beginning, middle and end.
7. Brandt identifies 3 levels of action in an anecdote:
   (i) Molar behaviour: e.g., Mary riding a bike
   (ii) Subordinate units: e.g., Mary riding a bike for the third time that morning.
   (iii) Molecular units: e.g., Mary riding a bike slowly around in circles.
8. Finally, in recording an anecdote, it is important to be accurate, objective and complete. It is better to record too much data than too little.

PRACTICAL EXERCISE TWO: AN ANECDOTAL RECORD

Introduction
In 1926 Jean Piaget published his observations and interpretations of children's reasoning in a book illustrated with anecdotes. The anecdotes were largely based on observation of his own children's behaviour. His theory of cognitive development

subsequently developed from observation of children has captured the interest of many child psychologists and started a wave of research that has continued unabated to this day. It is a dramatic illustration of how one method of child observation, carefully applied, can lead to important and insightful breakthroughs into our understanding of children's behaviour.

Procedure

The task of collecting anecdotes is a very lengthy one. One shortcut is to interview the parents of a number of children asking them to recount stories of their children's recent behaviour. By this means a number of anecdotal descriptions of aspects of children's behaviour will emerge. Another approach is to record the anecdotes yourself by talking with children. Here the idea might be to focus on one aspect of children's behaviour, e.g., cognitive or moral development, perhaps presenting them with a problem or dilemma to solve and recording their answers.

Questions to Consider

1. What new light did anecdotes throw on behaviour of children?
2. What are the advantages and disadvantages of the method?

SPECIMEN DESCRIPTIONS

Barker and Wright (1955) have pioneered the method which has come to be known as specimen description. The method was intended to be used in the study of behaviour in natural settings, where the observer was to avoid interfering with the ongoing stream of behaviour. The observer's task requires recording as fully as possible what is happening, the context within which it is happening and the people involved. The written account of the subject's ongoing behaviour is called a specimen record. Barker and Wright's (1955) study is an example of the use of the method to study everyday life in an American town.

To facilitate data analysis a number of categories have been developed to help interpret the behaviour in meaningful ways.

(i) Behaviour Episodes. These are units of behaviour that describe a particular situation and some ongoing behaviour in that setting.

(ii) Behaviour Setting. These units have been defined by Wright (1956, p.266) as "a stable part of the physical and social milieu of a community together with an attached standing pattern of behaviour". For example, in the Barker and Wright (1955) study of a mid-western town the number of hours citizens spent in the drug store, second-grade class room, tavern, etc., were identified.

In the following specimen description, (i) behaviour episodes and (ii) behaviour settings have been used to categorize the data.

Participants:	Sarah: Age 7 years	Date: 24/10/86
	Katie: Age 4 years	Observation Commenced: 2.05 p.m.
Setting:	Parents' home	Observation Finished: 2.20 p.m.

2.05	Sarah and Katie are playing at being "grown-ups" in the lounge-room of their parents' home. They are discussing their forthcoming participation in their favourite uncle's wedding.
EPISODE 1	Sarah (in a grown-up voice): "Mummy will paint my nails for the wedding."
	Katie says: "Me too."
	Sarah says rather disdainfully: "But you bite your nails and if mummy paints your nails and you meet people at the wedding they will look at your nails and say 'Look, that little girl bites her nails'."
2.10	Then Sarah says: "Come on - let's play in the bedroom." And they move to their bedroom to dress up and put makeup on. They take their dolls.
EPISODE 2	Sarah adopts the role of a grown-up named 'Judy' and Katie becomes another mother called 'Dianne'. Sarah in her grown-up voice says: "This is my baby and he is 11 weeks old."
2.15	Katie says: "This is my baby and he's just born and he is 21 months old - and I have just come home from hospital with him."
	Sarah (breaking the role play): "Oh! Katie - you can't have just come home from hospital with a 21 month old baby - your baby should be little and wrinkled."
EPISODE 2	Sarah says (resuming role play): "I'm going to feed my baby."
	Katie says: "I will feed my baby too."

Methods of Direct Observation

Advantages of Specimen Description
1. The method captures the full range, richness and complexity of behaviour.
2. The individual is studied in the natural setting.
3. The written record can be previewed as many times as necessary.
4. Only a minimal amount of equipment is required and so it is a relatively inexpensive method to use.

Disadvantages of Specimen Description
1. It is a time consuming method of observation given that the observations must be recorded, typed or written up and then coded.
2. Even with the aid of behaviour setting and behaviour episode codes it is difficult to accurately quantify the data.
3. Problems exist establishing the reliability of the observations.

Guidelines for Recording Specimen Descriptions
Wright (1960) presents the following guidelines for researchers interested in utilizing specimen descriptions:

1. Describe the scene exactly as viewed by the observer.
2. Focus closely on the subject's behaviour and whatever is affecting the behaviour.
3. Record as accurately as possible what the subject says and does.
4. Bracket all the interpretive material so that it stands out.
5. Describe how the subject behaves.
6. Describe how anyone interacts with the subject.
7. Be careful to record the order in which events occur.
8. Describe behaviour in terms of what is done rather than in relation to what is not done.
9. Keep descriptions simple and write in everyday language.
10. Mark off time intervals.

Methods of Direct Observation

PRACTICAL EXERCISE THREE: SPECIMEN DESCRIPTION

Introduction
Barker and Wright (1955), Wright (1967) and Barker
(1968) have written a number of books describing
studies they have conducted using the specimen
description method.   To obtain some insight into
how the method is used, it would be worthwhile
reading one or more of these books.

Procedure
Select a child and a time when the child can be
observed uninterrupted for 30 minutes.   Wright
(1960) suggests that observations be limited to 30
minutes in a single setting to avoid observer
fatigue.   The purpose of the observation is to
record the child's behaviour in its context, in
sufficient detail to facilitate examination of the
record at a later date.   The observation may be
collected using a notebook outlined in the
following way.

Today's date:
Time observation commenced:
Time recorded in 5 minute intervals
   9.30:   the child was playing with a
           group of friends in the school
           sand box
   9.35:
   9.40:

Having collected the specimen description,
type the notes out.   Using the categories of (i)
behaviour settings (ii) behaviour episodes, mark
out the specimen description accordingly.   To
assess the reliability of the coding use an
independent observer to code the narrative record
using the above two categories.   See Chapter 7 for
a description of the method for determining the
reliability of an observation.

Questions to Consider
1.   How difficult was it to categorize the
      narrative record into (i) behaviour settings
      and (ii) behaviour episodes? Did categorizing
      the data in this way help interpret the
      observations collected?   Were independent
      observers able to reliably identify the same

categories?
2. To what extent did the child(ren) react to the presence of the observer?

EVENT SAMPLING

Imagine a schoolyard setting at recess time - the yard is full of children milling about and the air full of the noise of their play. In twos and threes they race around in apparently meaningless fashion. In one corner of the yard a scuffle breaks out between two children and then ends as suddenly as it began. On a seat by the main building a lone child sits looking out on the playground. Faced with this very complex and ever changing picture how could a teacher or observer begin to record and make sense of the stream of behaviour before one's eyes.

One method for analysing the stream of behaviour is known as event sampling. Using this method an observer would focus on a specific act, e.g., quarrels between children in the playground or co-operative acts between children. The children would then be observed for a specific time period. For example, Dawe (1934) studied quarrelling among children in a pre-school setting. In her study there were 40 children aged between 25-60 months. From her 59 hours of observation, she noted among other things, a total of 200 quarrels, with males quarrelling more than females and most incidents lasting less than one minute.

Although still not as widely used as other sampling methods there is an increasing acceptance of the method as a means for recording observations. Technological breakthroughs have occurred in relation to both recording and analysing data.

Advantages of Event Sampling

1. Wright (1960, p.107) notes that event sampling "structures the field of observation into natural units of behaviour and situation. Event sampling preserves the context into which events fit". That is, the method retains or preserves the integrity of the situation and the events observed.

2. Another advantage of event sampling is that it is economical in terms of the time spent collecting the data.

3. A further strength of the method is that it can be used for either infrequently or frequently occurring behaviour whereas other methods such as time sampling are best used with frequently occurring behaviour.

Disadvantages of Event Sampling

1. Despite its advantages the method is not widely used in child study. Yarrow and Anderson (1979) believe that one reason it is not widely used, particularly in relation to parent-child relations, is that it does not really lend itself to the study of the way individuals respond to each other when interacting.

Guidelines for Event Sampling

1. Having decided that event sampling is the most appropriate method for sampling the stream of behaviour, the first task of the researcher is to carefully define the event(s) under study.
2. Careful consideration then needs to be given to the best setting in which to observe the behaviour under study. For example the school playground would provide the right setting for a study of children's quarrels or co-operative behaviour.
3. Some consideration is then needed of the kinds of questions one is interested in answering from the data as a preliminary step to determining your recording method. For example, one might tape record observations from which typed transcriptions could be made. Alternative methods include video-recordings or recording sheets. A review of the various methods for recording behaviour is provided in Chapter 6. If a recording sheet is used consideration needs to be given to information about the event that needs to be recorded. Thus information might be recorded about:

1. duration of the event
2. content, i.e., what was said/done and to whom
3. context of event, i.e., where event occurred and

4. outcome, i.e., what followed after the event.

An example of a recording sheet is provided below where the event under study is quarrels among pre-school children. The setting is the pre-school playground at lunchtime. A quarrel is defined as "a disagreement or argument between children involving verbal or non-verbal behaviour".

Quarrel	Duration	No. chn. involved	Sex of chn.	Context	Outcome
1	2.0 mins.	2	M & F	Sandbox	1 cried & left.
2	2.4 mins.	3	2M,1F	Sandbox	F left.
3	2.3 mins.	2	2F	Cubby-house	Remained in house.

PRACTICAL EXERCISE FOUR: EVENT SAMPLING

Introduction
The aim of this study is to observe children's play behaviour.

Method
Subjects
Observe a group (10-20) of young school children in a school setting (Age range 5-10 years).

Procedure
Before beginning the observation, familiarize yourself with the children and with the school setting. It is important that the children accept your presence as an observer. Choose a general free play activity period for observation when there is a minimum of adult structuring of the situation.
Observe each child in turn for 3 minutes. Follow the alphabetical list of names so that your decision concerning which child to observe is not influenced by the occurrence of social interaction at that time. Place a check under the appropriate column for each play contact as it occurs during a 3 minute interval.
Observe on three different days so that each child is observed for a total of nine minutes. The separate days of observation will permit an

43

estimate of the consistency of children's play behaviour from one day to the next and will help to guard against the possibility that certain factors were present on a single day that altered or distorted the typical social interactions of the children. For example, the number of children as well as which particular children are present on a given day may affect the kinds of play behaviour which occurs.

The following behaviours will serve to define the play events observed:

Solitary Play: The child is playing alone and attention is not directed toward another child either for the purpose of attracting attention or as a disruptive act. For example, the child is kicking a football around the oval by him or herself.

Parallel Play: To score this event the child's play mimics that of another child without there being a verbal or non-verbal exchange. For example, a child is playing with some blocks while another nearby group of children is also playing with blocks.

Co-operative Play: The child is engaged in sharing or co-operative play with another child or group of children. For example, the children are completing a jigsaw puzzle.

Aggressive Play: The child is engaged in rough and tumble play involving pushing, scuffling, wrestling or vigorous physical contact. For example the child wrestles another child to the floor.

Other Play: This category is scored for any other form of play that cannot be accommodated by the preceding categories.

Below is an example of the kind of recording sheet you might use for recording your observations. Adapt and develop the recording sheet as necessary.

Methods of Direct Observation

Observation Schedule

General activity _____ Date _____

Number of children present _____ Time _____

Children's Names   Play Categories
                          Solitary   Parallel   Co-operative   Other
Anderson, J.
Ball, T.
Carrington, J.
Dalton, L.

Discussion Questions

1. Were there any difficulties in reliably identifying categories of play in children?
2. Would another method such as specimen description or time sampling be a more appropriate means for recording your observations?
3. What were the advantages and disadvantages of event sampling?

TIME SAMPLING

Faced with the problem of sampling the stream of behaviour it is possible to consider sampling as either (a) time independent, i.e., event sampling or (b) time dependent. Simply put, a time dependent procedure involves dividing the behaviour stream into arbitrary time intervals with each interval being scored for the presence or absence of the designated behaviour. In turn, a time dependent method may be categorized as either (i) one-zero sampling or (ii) continuous recording.

(i) The time sampling method involves observing for a specified time interval and then taking time out to record the behaviour. For example, in their study, Yarrow, Rubenstein and Pedersen (1975) observed for 30 seconds and recorded to 60 seconds. There are no guidelines for determining the intervals over which behaviours are observed or recorded. Altman (1974) in a review of sampling methods is heavily critical of one-zero sampling noting that it arbitrarily segments the stream of behaviour with a resultant loss of continuity, sequencing and patterning of behaviour.

(ii) With the advent of film and video recording in child study, the method of continuous recording has attained considerable popularity. The method involves recording the presence or absence of behaviour during arbitrarily selected time intervals. The difference between this method and one-zero sampling is that because behaviours are coded from a permanent record, e.g., video, no time out is needed to record behaviour. Yarrow and Anderson (1979) note that, with continuous recording, information is available on the (i) frequency, (ii) concurrence and (iii) sequencing of behaviour.

Frequency. Time sampling has been used quite extensively in determining the frequency of occurrence of various behaviours, including verbal and non-verbal behaviour (Lewis and Lee-Painter, 1974; Anderson and Vietze, 1977; Russell, 1983) and emotional expression (Wimberger and Kogan, 1968; Slee, 1984).

An important issue which does arise with the use of time sampling concerns whether or not the method provides an accurate measure of the frequency of behaviour. The issue arises because the procedure usually adopted with time sampling is to score a behaviour only once per time interval regardless of how many times it actually occurs during the interval. Basically, the two important factors which affect whether or not time sampling provides an accurate record of the frequency of behaviour concern how often the behaviour stream is sampled and whether the behaviours are considered as events or states.

In relation to the first factor Powell, Martindale and Kulp (1975) found that the more frequently the sample measures were made, the closer did the scores obtained reflect the actual frequency of the behaviour as it occurred in "real time". They found that a 10 second time sampling interval provided a far more accurate estimate of the frequency of a child's "in seat" school behaviour than did a 60 second interval.

The other factor which contributes to the

extent to which time sampling can provide an accurate assessment of the frequency with which a behaviour occurs concerns the nature of the behaviour under study. Altman (1974) distinguishes between behaviours considered as events and those considered as states. Altman considers events to be instantaneous while states have appreciable duration. If the behaviour under study has some appreciable duration then it is possible that time sampling may provide a good estimate of the frequency with which it occurs. This will be the case when the actual length of the sampling interval is shorter than the duration of the behaviour (Sackett, 1978).

To summarize then, it has been argued here that time sampling can provide an accurate frequency measure if the behaviour stream is sampled frequently and if the time interval used is shorter than the average duration of the behaviour.

Concurrence. Time sampling is also a useful method to employ when the researcher is interested in examining concurrent or simultaneous behaviour. Thus Brazelton, Tronick, Adamson, Als and Wise (1975) have used this method to examine the intensity or level of activity in mother-infant interaction. In other research, Lewis and Lee-Painter (1974) in discussing the use of time sampling to measure simultaneous behaviour note that it "provides some idea of the amount of general mother-infant interaction, and, by looking at the ratio of total frequency of behaviour to simultaneous behaviours, a general environment responsivity score can be obtained" (p.31).

Sequencing. Finally, it is possible to use time sampling to investigate the sequential nature of particular behaviours during interaction. Basically, sequential analysis involves investigating the occurrence of any particular behaviour following the occurrence of any identified target behaviour. For example, Parke (1978) uses this method in a study of mother-infant interaction. He found that the probability of the parent ceasing to feed the infant in response to an infant auditory distress signal was .33 whereas the unconditional probability (chance occurrence) of this parent behaviour was quite low (.05). Slee (1983,b, 1984) has used sequential analysis to investigate the nature of mother-infant vocal and gaze interaction. In both studies, continuous sampling of 5 second intervals was the method used to score mothers' and infants' vocalizations and gaze activity. Overall then, time sampling offers the researcher an important means for investigating behaviour. In choosing to use the method though, one other important issue to consider concerns the length of the sampling interval to employ.

Choosing a Sampling Interval

An examination of the literature shows that time sampling is used quite extensively. Considerable variation exists in the length of intervals used. For example Stern (1974) used an interval of 0.6 second; Anderson and Vietze (1977) = 1 second; Lewis and Lee-Painter (1974) = 10 seconds; Richards and Bernal (1971) = 30 seconds. As Yarrow and Anderson (1979, p.216) note there are as yet "no guidelines for determining the cycle for observing and recording or the length of time most appropriate for sampling parent-infant interactive behaviour".

Consequently, with the notable exception of Lewis and Lee-Painter (1974), it is difficult to find instances where researchers have provided a rationale for the interval used in their time-sampling method. Lewis and Lee-Painter (1974) in their analysis of mother-infant interactive behaviour chose a 10 second interval because "too short a time base and very few behaviours would be classified as interactive, while too long a time base would include all behaviours in one long interaction, wherein specific behaviour categories would become blurred" (p.31). As indicated in their statement, the primary determinant in the choice of a particular time interval was the nature of the behaviour under investigation.

In summary then, in choosing a time sampling interval, consideration should be given to the questions being asked of the data and the nature of the behaviours being observed. If the data is to be used to assess the frequency with which behaviours occur then the time intervals should be small to enhance the accuracy of the frequency estimates. Similarly, the behaviours would be preferably of some duration rather than instantaneous in order to enhance accuracy in frequency estimates.

Methods of Direct Observation

Advantages of Time Sampling
1. It is an efficient and time saving method of collecting data.
2. Time sampling can be used for measuring discrete behaviours such as vocalization or gaze or with rating scales in the measurement of behaviours such as emotional expression.
3. Time sampling lends itself to the investigation of various aspects of behaviour including frequency and concurrence and to sequential analysis.

Disadvantages of Time Sampling
1. Time sampling is best used with behaviours that occur relatively frequently.
2. The method arbitrarily segments the stream of behaviour into artificial time segments.
3. Some writers have expressed serious reservations about its use particularly as a frequency measure.

Guidelines for Time Sampling
1. Time sampling is appropriate for behaviours that occur fairly frequently. It has been successfully applied in the study of vocal (Rosenthal, 1982; Slee, 1983,b), gaze (Gunnar & Donahue, 1980; Slee, 1984) and emotional expression (Gaensbauer, Mrazek & Emde, 1979).
2. Time sampling is best used for behaviours that are readily identifiable.
3. Care should be taken to define the behaviour(s) under study to facilitate their reliable identification.
4. In choosing a sampling interval, consideration should be given to the purpose of the study. If frequency measures are to be obtained care must be taken to choose an interval that is sufficiently short to provide an accurate measure.
5. Consideration must also be given to whether the sampling will be continuous in nature or whether a method such as one-zero sampling can be used.

Methods of Direct Observation

PRACTICAL EXERCISE FIVE: TIME SAMPLING

Introduction
The present exercise was taken from a study by Yarrow, Rubenstein and Pedersen (1975) entitled "Infant and Environment: Early cognitive and motivational development".

The purpose of the study was to investigate the nature of infant's early home environment as a means for developing intervention programs to optimize the environment of young infants. In the exercise the purpose is to use a time sampling method (one-zero) to collect data on mother-infant interaction in the natural home environment (See Yarrow et al's paper).

Method
Subjects
The two infants chosen for the study should be 5-6 months of age. If possible, mothers should be chosen from contrasting economic status groups, i.e., one from a high and one from a low socio-economic group.

Observation Procedures
Each mother-infant pair should be observed once. The time sampling cycle consists of a 30 second observation period and a 60 second recording period. During the observations which last for one hour, the mother is asked to continue with her normal household routine and not communicate with the observer.

Observer Reliability
Prior to commencing observations, the categories need to be checked for reliability. Two observers should simultaneously code mother-infant inter-action in the home for a period of 15 minutes. Reliability coefficients can be calculated according to the procedure outlined in Chapter 7.

Observation Categories
In the present exercise, only a limited number of behaviours will be scored for mothers and infants. These are outlined below:

Infant Behaviours

Vocalization   All sounds, positive, neutral and negative except coughs, and breathing.
   (i)   Positive: cooing; burbling/babbling (P+)
   (ii) Negative: crying (N-)

Visual attention The infant looks directly at the person's face or body.

Fleeting glances are not scored.

(i) Gaze can be directed at mother

(ii) Gaze directed to another person

Maternal Behaviours

Vocalization

(i) Vocalization to infant (V-I)

(ii) Vocalization to infant following infant's non-distress vocalization (VOC+)

(iii) Vocalization to infant following infant's distress vocalization (VOC-)

(iv) Imitative vocalization when mother imitates infant sound (Im).

Visual Attention

(i) The mother looks at the infant's face or body

(ii) Mutual visual regard when mother and infant look at each other.

These categories are scored using recording sheets drawn up as follows:

Subject _____ Time Observations Commenced _____
Observer _____ Time Observations Finished _____
Today's date _____

	Infant Behaviours				Mother Behaviour			
	Vocal		Visual		Vocal			Visual
Time Block	P+	N-	Look M.	Look Other	V-I	Voc+	Im.	Look I.	Mut. Vis.
1									
2									
3									
4									
5									
6									

<u>Questions to Consider</u>
1. How easy was it to record mother's and infant's behaviour reliably?
2. What problems, if any, were experienced with the one-zero time sampling method? Is there a more appropriate time sampling method for the behaviours under study here?

<u>RATING SCALES</u>

As Brandt (1972, p.118) states, "perhaps the most prevalent type of observational data within the behavioural sciences is the rating, a judgement made about the degree or extent of some human characteristic." Basically a rating scale is a measuring instrument that involves an observer assigning a particular numerical or descriptive value to a rated object. The common characteristic of rating scales concerns the concept of a continuum where a "... judge is asked to evaluate and allocate samples along this continuum at a sequential array of way points" (Horrocks, 1964, p.573).
   The two main types of rating scales are called (1) graphic and (ii) numerical, being substantively similar and differing mainly in detail.

   (i) <u>Graphic</u>

   very   hungry   not hungry   not at all
   hungry   hungry

   In graphic scales the intervals are combined with descriptive phrases.

   (ii) <u>Numerical</u>
   Rate how hungry you are from (1) very hungry to (4) not at all hungry on the following scale:

   1   2   3   4

   Numerical scales are easy to construct and amenable to statistical analysis.

   Overall, opinion is somewhat divided as to the relative merits of rating scales in observational research. Oppenheim (1966) is very critical of their use, suggesting that their primary weakness arises from the raters themselves. Thus,

difficulties arise where observers are too
generous in their ratings (error of leniency),
where the scores cluster near the centre of the
scale (error of central tendency) or where their
ratings are unduly biased (halo effect).
Brandt (1972) suggests that another weakness
of rating scales relates to the ambiguity or
imprecise nature of the trait being measured. For
example, what one observer may view as "aggressive"
behaviour another may not. As such, the global
diffuse nature of the quality being measured makes
the task of rating a difficult one. Brandt also
notes that another problem of rating scales
concerns the assumption that the quality or trait
being measured is consistent across time and
situation and such an assumption is not always
warranted.

Alternatively, other researchers have argued
that rating scales possess advantages that justify
their use in observational studies. Kerlinger
(1973) notes that some of these advantages include
their time saving nature, ease of use and wide
range of application. More recently, a number of
writers have argued that rating scales are more
useful than discrete behavioural observations for
the investigation of certain aspects of behaviour.
For example, Waters (1978), Clarke-Stewart and
Hevey (1981) and Slee (1984,b) argue that rating
scales are particularly useful for assessing the
stability of behaviour. Kogan (1970) has noted
that rating scales are useful for assessing the
characteristic features or style of an individual's
behaviour.

In summary, researchers have come to recognize
that despite their potential weaknesses, rating
scales have an important role to play in
observational research. Indeed, for certain types
of research questions, rating scales may be more
applicable than the observation of discrete
behaviour.

Advantages of Rating Scales
1. Important advantages of rating scales
   include their ease of construction and
   relative ease of use.
2. A related advantage is that rating scales
   can be used by people with a minimum of
   training.
3. Rating scales are particularly suitable
   for measuring aspects of behaviour that
   are not readily quantifiable, e.g.,

expressions of emotion/affect.
4. They also have important application in the measurement of the stability of behaviour over time.

Disadvantages of Rating Scales

Kerlinger (1973) argues that there are both extrinsic and intrinsic weaknesses associated with rating scales:
1. Extrinsically they are seemingly so easy to construct and use that they are often used indiscriminately.
2. Intrinsically, rating scales are liable to biased error in relation to (i) error of leniency, (ii) error of central tendency and (iii) halo effect.

Guidelines for Rating Scales

1. As Oppenheim (1966) noted, in developing and using a rating scale the first step is to define the dimension being rated. The dimension should have approximately the same meaning to all those using it. Oppenheim recommends that an uneven number of steps be used in the scale and that the number of steps be less than 10. Raters usually find it difficult to make discriminations finer than 10 points.
2. Having identified the dimension and the number of steps involved, consideration then needs to be given to defining each step. The descriptions of each point will facilitate raters' discriminations.
3. Rating scales should only be used for the investigation of certain research problems.

I HAVE ONE SMALL QUERY ABOUT YOUR RATING SCALE — ON WHAT BASIS DO YOU DISCRIMINATE BETWEEN NO 8.— "MILD FRUITY" AND NO 9.— "REALLY FREAKED OUT"?

PRACTICAL EXERCISE SIX: RATING SCALES

Introduction

Slee (1982, 1983,a,b, 1984) has developed a rating
scale for the study of emotional expression in
infants and mothers. The 5 point scale involves
rating mothers and infants in terms of
"affectionate", "warm", "neutral", "cold" and
"hostile" emotional expression. In various reviews
of the literature the "affectionate-hostile"
dimension has been identified as a significant
component of the mother-infant relationship (Slee,
1983,a). Moreover, researchers such as Kogan et al
(1969) have successfully used the dimension to
rate mothers' and children's emotional
expressions. In using the present rating scale
the observer makes global judgements of the mother
or child's emotional expression. This involves
the observer empathising as fully as possible with
the subject while taking into account the context
in which the emotions arise and the attendant
verbal and non-verbal behaviours. Reliability for
the rating scales averages 0.84.

Method

Choose 3-5 infants for the study aged between 6
months and 18 months.

Observation Procedure

The observations should be made in the mothers'
own homes. Select a period of time when the
infant will be awake and make your observations
during (i) feeding time, (ii) free play time where
each observation lasts for 10 minutes providing 20
minutes in all. During the free play time ask the
mother to play with her infant as she normally
does. Using a time sampling procedure observe the
infant for 1 minute and then rate the infant for
emotional expression using the descriptions
provided below. Ten ratings should be obtained
for feeding and for free play.

The Rating Scale

Mothers' Emotional Expression

Affectionate

The affectionate category is scored for the
mother's joyful, excited or exuberant interaction
with her infant. The feeling generated by the
mother is one of complete emotional and physical

absorption in the infant. There is usually an element of liveliness, excitement or vigour associated with affectionate emotional quality.

Warm
Warm emotional expression is scored for the mother's sensitive concern and caring for the infant. Warm emotional quality conveys the feeling that the mother accepts and understands the infant's feelings and behaviour and her behaviour communicates this feeling to the infant. Her involvement with the infant is non-evaluative and non-critical and there is a certain tenderness associated with her interaction with the infant.

Neutral
Neutral emotion is scored for those interactive sequences where the mother's involvement with the infant is of a more routine and practical nature. The mother appears tolerant of the infant's behaviour but her involvement lacks animation and feeling. Her general attitude may appear somewhat distractible and if she is involved in some task of caring for the infant she may appear as more concerned with completing the task. Overall her behaviour indicates some disregard or indifference to the feelings of the infant.

Cold
Mother's cold emotional expression invokes a feeling of haste, urgency or impatience. Her involvement with the infant tends to be mildly directive, authoritarian or interfering, i.e. the mother tends to initiate or structure the situation to meet her own requirements or needs rather than those of the infant. The behaviour of the mother suggests that she is controlling or attempting to control the situation and in some instances she may convey a note of dissatisfaction or disapproval of the infant's behaviour.

Hostile
The hostile emotional category is scored where the mother's involvement with the infant is openly rejecting, controlling or disapproving. Basically the mother is imposing her own will and ignoring or rejecting the feelings and needs of the infant. The mother's actions suggest that she may act to change or direct the behaviour of the infant. The general feeling generated during hostile emotional expression is one of strain or tension.

Infants' Emotional Expression

Affectionate
The affectionate category is scored for the infant's joyful, excited or happy behaviour. The infant's behaviour is expressive, lively and animated in nature and he literally does "jump for joy" when in this state. The feeling generated by the infant's behaviour is one of intensity and vigour.

Warm
Warm emotional expression is scored for those interactive sequences with the mother which are pleasurable and harmonious in nature. The infant's actions create feelings of contentment and enjoyment and the infant's general demeanour is one of alert activity and responsiveness. During warm emotional expression his behaviour suggests that he is open and receptive to interaction.

Neutral
Neutral emotional expression is scored for those interactive sequences where the infant demonstrates or shows a minimal amount of emotional involvement with the mother. The feelings generated by the infant's behaviour and attitude during such sequences is that he is only minimally affected by the interaction and is more concerned with his own activities. Generally the infant appears to be emotionally distant and unresponsive or distractible during neutral emotional quality.

Cold
Cold emotional expression may be described as negative or suffering behaviour. The infant's behaviour generates a feeling of unhappiness or discomfort. Cold emotional expression could also be described in terms of impatience or annoyance arising out of some apparent frustration. Generally there is a rather abrasive quality associated with cold emotional expression.

Hostile
Hostile emotional expression is scored for angry, rejecting or distressed communication with the mother. Loud and continuous distress signals or tantrum behaviour are more specific features associated with hostile emotion. An important aspect of hostile emotional expression is its intense nature. The general feeling generated by the infant's behaviour is one of intense unhappiness, discomfort or frustration.

Reliability
If possible have a second observer also rate the
infant for emotional expression. Calculate the
reliability of the scale using the procedure
outlined in Chapter 7.

Questions to Consider
1. How reliable were the ratings?
2. Is a rating scale the most appropriate
   method for assessing emotional expression
   in infants?
3. Was a 1 minute time interval the most
   appropriate time interval for rating?

CHAPTER SUMMARY
In this chapter a number of the most commonly used
methods for recording observations have been
described and their advantages and disadvantages
identified. In choosing to use a particular
method, factors to keep in mind include:

- the purpose for which the observations
  are being made and more particularly the
  questions being asked in the study
- the nature of the behaviour under study,
  e.g., discrete identifiable behaviours
  such as verbal or non-verbal behaviour or
  more subjective, interpretive behaviour
  such as feeling states
- the statistical analysis to be performed
  on the data.

In Table 4.1 summary descriptions of the
methods used for recording observations reviewed
in this chapter are outlined.

Table 4.1. Summary Description of Methods for Recording Observations

Method of Observation	Summary Description	Advantages	Disadvantages
1. Baby Biographies	A diary-type account of children's behaviour.	Identifies development over time. Provides a rounded description of behaviour.	Problems with observer bias. Difficulties in separating out interpretation and observation.

Methods of Direct Observation

2. Anecdotal Observations	Involves observation of specific incidents of behaviour e.g., imitative behaviour.	Easy method to employ. Helps generate hypotheses.	Time consuming. Problems with reliability.
3. Specimen Description	Involves observation of behaviour in natural settings.	The method captures the richness of behaviour. The child is studied in the natural setting. Requires minimal equipment.	Time consuming. Difficult to quantify data. Problems with reliability.
4. Event Sampling	Requires the observation of a specific act, e.g., quarrels.	The method preserves the context of behaviour. Suitable for use with infrequently occurring behaviour.	Problems exist with capturing the sequencing of behaviour.
5. Time Sampling	Divides the stream of behaviour into intervals with intervals scored for behaviour. Types include (i) one-zero, (ii) continuous sampling.	An economical and efficient method. Amenable to statistical analysis.	Best used with frequently occurring behaviour. The method involves artificial segmentation of the behaviour stream.
6. Rating Scales	Involves assigning a numerical or descriptive value to a rated object.	Easily constructed and used. Requires minimal training. Suitable for measuring behaviour not amenable to quantification.	Liable to errors of leniency, central tendency and halo effect.

Chapter Five

THE NEW HERMENEUTIC

Could a greater miracle take place than for us
to look through each other's eyes for an
instant? We should live in all the ages of
the world in an hour; ay, in all the worlds
of the ages. History, Poetry, Mythology! -- I
know of no reading of another's experience so
startling and informing as this would be
(Thoreau, 1960, p.12).

INTRODUCTION
There is currently considerable upheaval occurring
in the way the social sciences conceive of, and
conduct research. "In all the social sciences,
traditional methodologies are seemingly being
challenged" (Bullivant, 1978, p.240). Exciting
new developments are occurring across the spectrum
of the social sciences as new paradigms are
emerging. As noted in Chapter 1, a paradigm
provides the means for circumscribing how
scientists can meaningfully use terms like
"knowledge" and "science", identifies the nature
of theories used in research, the problems worthy
of investigation, and the methods used to
investigate the problems. Presently, paradigm
shifts are occurring in relation to education
(Young, 1981); psychology (Manicas & Secord,
1983; Reason & Rowan, 1981); and social welfare
(DeMaria, 1981; Battye & Slee, 1985) to cite but
a few examples.
Impetus for the paradigm shift is arising from
a growing disenchantment by the scientific
community with the assumptions about the supposed
power and infallibility of the natural scientific
method upon which mainstream social sciences are
based. Writers from a variety of disciplines
including psychology (Viney, 1985; Battye & Slee,
1985) and education (Bullivant, 1978) are

challenging researchers to adopt a more flexible approach in their research endeavours, a flexibility that would not be so constrained by assumptions inherent in the natural scientific method. In this chapter, consideration is given to describing the way people conceive of science and the world around them. This discussion will provide an entré into the task of understanding basic tenets of the natural scientific method and understanding the new heuristic in the social sciences, namely hermeneutics. Consideration will be given to the role of observation in the hermeneutic approach and illustrative educational and psychological studies which have employed an hermeneutic methodology will be described.

WAYS OF KNOWING
In order to understand the role of the paradigm shift, some description of the way people conceive of, and think about science is necessary. One influential framework for understanding how people perceive the world around them that has provided considerable impetus for research was conceived by Carl Jung. As described by Fordham (1971), Jung's model encompasses the two independent dimensions of thinking-feeling and sensing-intuition. In Jung's view, thinking people apply their intellectual faculties in trying to adapt themselves to people and circumstance. Feeling people find their way in terms of value judgements. Sensing people focus attention on detail and specifics of a situation and tend to be practical and realistic. Intuitive individuals rely more on their imagination and are idealistic and interested in hypothetical viewpoints.

One attempt to operationalise Jung's typologies was undertaken by Royce (1964) who identified by interview, four clusters of beliefs that people hold about science. The clusters included (i) rationalism-thinking (ii) empiricism-thinking (iii) intuition-feeling and (iv) authoritarianism-believing. Unfortunately, research failed to verify these categories (Jones, 1963).

Tomkins (1966), a psychologist, included a number of epistemological items in a 57-item scale for measuring basic orientations in western thought. Tomkins found some evidence for clusters of attitudes about science related to beliefs of people that human beings are basically good or evil. A belief in the goodness of people was

61

found to be associated with attitudes about science that stressed an individual's activity, capacity for invention, and the excitement of discovery. A belief that people are basically evil was associated with attitudes about science that stressed the importance of separating reality from fantasy, the vulnerability of humans to delusion and error and the necessity for objectivity and detachment.

Young (1981) in an insightful study into teachers' views of knowledge, found that the majority of teachers either held a logical-empiricist view or gave priority to more subjective or intuitive ways of knowing. A small minority of his sample possessed a dualistic system in which both views of knowledge were held. About 10% of his sample could not be classified using his typology.

Battye and Slee (1985) have developed a theoretical model for understanding the way people view knowledge. The four positions in their model flow from the traditional is (facts) - ought (values) distinction of moral philosophy. In their model, a person's adoption of an epistemological position depends upon (i) the nature of the activity or the information sought and (ii) the nature of the final authority. That is, each position presupposes a particular understanding of the philosophy of science and valuing activity. Moreover, inherent in each position is a particular view of the person, particularly in relation to the issue of "agency". As noted in Chapter 3, "agency" is an important and central feature of new paradigm research. To reiterate, an agent is someone who takes responsibility for his/her behaviour, is understood as being capable of acting for certain purposes or goals, attaches some freedom of choice to the acts and may cite reasons for behaviour, reasons which are often guided by values. The four positions in the Battye and Slee model include:

> Position 1   which is identified by an appeal to values only. Advocates of this position are sometimes referred to as mystics or anti-scientists. As argued by Battye and Slee, in its most extreme form adoption of this position denies a person's agency because

	it conceives of humans simply as an extension of nature.
Position 2	which is characterised by a recognition of a person's values, but the final arbiter of what constitutes knowledge is an appeal to facts.
Position 3	which is identified by a recognition of facts, but in contrast to position 2 the final determinant of what constitutes valid knowledge involves values.
Position 4	is typically known as the mechanistic or positivist stance and is characterised by an appeal to facts only. In the mechanist view the individual is seen as a reactive/passive organism.

As argued by Battye and Slee (1985), position 3 best allows for the agency/reflexivity of the person. This is not to imply that social scientists may not combine two or more of the four positions or move from one approach to another. However, the strength of position 3 is that it acknowledges the post empiricist critique of science ... "namely, the value-ladeness of facts (facts are theory laden)... and the underdetermination of theory by facts ... Social science may be seen as value-laden ... and yet scientific (because it is nevertheless constrained by empirical data)" (Lyon, 1982, p.17).

Within position 3 it is accepted that social scientists are faced with the twin problems of (i) preinterpreted data and (ii) selection of the data for analysis. The hermeneutic or interpretive approach to human sciences has a number of advocates including Manicas and Secord (1983) and DeMaria (1981). As noted by Manicas and Secord (1983, p.410):

> ...it is by now commonplace that there is no such thing as a noninterpreted 'given' that can serve as a foundation of knowledge. This applies not only as regards our knowledge of the other person as agent, but also to our understanding of the natural world as well. That is, all our perceptions, categories, and frames of meaning are mediated, and are culturally and historically loaded.

As noted in Chapter 3 important aspects of the hermeneutic outlook include the view of people as (i) reflexive agents and (ii) a recognition that behaviour is embedded in context. One school of qualitative social research, ethnomethodology, includes the reflexivity of the subjects or actors, but tends to exclude the reflexivity of the observer or scientist, whereas the European hermeneutic school takes account of both forms of reflexivity. "In addition, if reflexivity mediated values are implicit in the concepts, methods and applications of all scientists, then it is perhaps better to make them explicit than to ignore them and have them come creeping back unannounced and unaccounted for" (Van Leeuwen, 1982, p.43).

That social science can be equated with hermeneutic science is a view shared by those researchers who lay stress on the articulation of world views of both investigators and actors. From an hermeneutic perspective, the world views that an individual employs are critical in understanding human behaviour.

Presently then, there is an identifiable body of literature concerned with understanding how people view and attempt to understand the world around them. Recent developments in the philosophy of science have witnessed the emergence of a more hermeneutic outlook in attempting to understand human behaviour. Underpinning the new hermeneutic is an emphasis on the agency of an individual and the contextual embeddedness of behaviour. The development of this new hermeneutic is associated with paradigm shifts in disciplines such as psychology and education. These paradigm shifts have important implications for how social scientists conceive of, and conduct research.

Interestingly, what we appear to be witnessing in the social sciences is the emergence of a "middle-ground methodology - partly quantitative - partly qualitative" (Bullivant, 1978, p.240). This argument also appears in a paper by Manicas and Secord (1983, p. 405) who note that "... once we are clearer about the nature of the sciences, we can see that psychology is best construed as a family of related sciences with different tasks and different methodologies." Their viewpoint is further developed when they observe that "Not all of psychology, however, is experimental psychology, and not all psychologists need to have the same tasks and methods" (Manicas & Secord, p.407). It is to the issue of the nature of observation in hermeneutic research that attention now turns.

THE NATURE OF OBSERVATION IN HERMENEUTIC RESEARCH

Direct observation is the archetypical technique of scientific enquiry in virtually every field of research. In seeking to explain or understand some phenomenon, the best procedure is usually to look at it closely and repeatedly. Certainly, direct observation is virtually indispensable for gathering certain types of data. Thus, where people are unaware of their behaviour, direct observation is a critical means for gathering information. Observational techniques are also most useful where people will not communicate details about their behaviour. For example, where people are strongly motivated to distort their behaviour or elevate their status (e.g., committing delinquent acts) direct observation may be a more useful technique to employ than alternative methods such as interviewing. However, the nature of the observational process as conceived by the natural scientific method differs from that employed in hermeneutic research.

From the perspective of a natural scientific method, emphasis is given to viewing events externally. The observer or experimenter is considered as a neutral, non-participating, objective professional who should minimise the impact of the observations on the subjects and who manipulates variables in a predetermined manner. Gary Zukav (1979, p.55) notes that:

The concept of scientific objectivity rests upon the assumption of an external world which is "out there" as opposed to an "I" which is "in here" (This way of perceiving, which puts other people "out there" makes it very lonely "in here"). According to this view, Nature in all her diversity is "out there". The task of the scientist is to observe the "out there" as objectively as possible. To observe something objectively means to see it as it would appear to an observer who has no prejudices about what he observes.

Scientific objectivity then, emphasises the need to minimise the effect of the observer on the subject's behaviour. Thus, Johnson and Bolstadt

(1973) have identified four sources of reactivity to an observer's presence including (i) the conspicuousness of the observer (ii) individual differences to being observed (iii) personal attributes of the observer and (iv) whether or not a rationale has been provided for the observations. Where reactivity to an observer's presence is noted, Johnson and Bolstadt recommend that efforts be made to adopt strategies that will minimise the effect of the observer on the subject's behaviour.

However, the view that science is an objective enterprise has been hotly disputed by science historian Kuhn (1970), philosophers Toulmin (1972); Polanyi (1964) and psychologists London (1964); Strupp and Hadley (1977). Trenchant criticism is currently being directed at the notion that science is, or can be, a value free neutral endeavour carried out by detached observers. For example, it is now better understood that the absolutely neutral or detached observer does not exist. Despite the claims of the logical positivists that an objective reality exists, it is now better understood that the world a person actually experiences cannot be totally objective. Our experience of the world occurs through a mutual interaction of observer and observed and our sensation of "reality" arises out of this interaction. Moreover, recent advances in the field of quantum physics emphasise the true extent of the misconception that the scientific endeavour is in any way a neutral, objective enterprise (Capra, 1982; Davies, 1982).

From an hermeneutic perspective, it is argued that there is no such thing as non-interpreted "brute-data". Our understanding and knowledge of persons and the world is mediated in relation to paradigms or world views. Emphasis is given to gaining an "inside" view of the person and understanding the world from the person's viewpoint. As Manicas and Secord (1983, p.409) note, in order to understand a person "... we must grasp the person's meanings and understandings, the agent's vision of the world, his or her plans, purposes, motivations and interests". Such information requires the use and development of research methods which facilitate gaining such a view. To this end, unstructured interviews and life histories provide important information. But it is participant observation that is widely mooted as the best means for obtaining an inside view.

Participant observation enables the research
worker to secure his data within the mediums,
symbols and experiential worlds which have
meaning to his respondents. Its intent is to
prevent imposing alien meanings upon the
actions of the subjects. Anthropologists
dealing with cultures other than their own
have consciously recognised and utilised the
techniques as a matter of necessity.
Experimental psychologists who try their own
instruments out on themselves as well as
psychiatrists who undergo analysis are
practising a form of participant observation
for much the same purposes as the
anthropologist (Vidich, 1955, p.354).

Participant observation is a rather broad term
including as it does, the data gathering
strategies of direct observation and general
interviewing in its armatarium. In this chapter,
concern lies with describing direct observation
procedures utilised in participant observation.
The literature is replete with definitions and
descriptions of the approach. However, the
definition of Schwartz and Schwartz (1955) seems
most consistent with the European hermeneutic
tradition.

For our purposes we define participant
observation as a process in which the
observer's presence in a social situation is
maintained for the purpose of scientific
investigation. The observer is in a face-
to-face relationship with the observed, and
by participating with them in their natural
life setting, he gathers data. Thus, the
observer is part of the context being observed,
and he both modifies and is influenced by this
context. The role of participant-observer may
be either formal or informal, concealed or
revealed; the observer may spend a good deal
or very little time in the research situation;
the participant-observer may be an integral
part of the social situation or largely
peripheral to it (p.344).

As is evident from the above definition, there
are a number of significant differences between
the nature of observation used in participant
observation and in the natural sciences. These
differences relate primarily to separating out

what is observed from the observer. Consideration is now given to a number of major concerns which arise when using participant observation including (i) the nature of the observational process (ii) data collection (iii) methods for recording data (iv) data retrieval and (v) reliability and validity of the data.

The Nature of the Observational Process

As a general rule, and as reflected in the definition of participant observation of Schwartz and Schwartz (1955) given earlier, the participant observer would typically spend some time in the field observing, interviewing and collecting data on all facets of the problem under investigation. The endeavour here would be to familiarise oneself with the situation and obtain as complete an understanding of the informant's (subject's) world and its meanings for him or her, as distinct from the observer's outer reconstructed view. The amount of time the observer would devote to immersion in the actual situation might vary from a few days or weeks to a year or more. Gold (1958) has developed a typology of the roles a researcher can adopt in participant observation including:

1. Complete participant: where the true identity and purpose of the observer is unknown. The observer may for example, work in a factory to learn about the inner workings of informal groups, without revealing to fellow workers that they are being studied.

2. Participant-as-observer: where the observer and informant are aware that they are observing and being observed. In this role the observer may switch between formally observing and data collection and informal observation as in attending and participating in meetings and parties.

3. Observer-as-participant: here the observations are more formal and contact with the informant is usually brief.

4. Complete observer: in this role the observer does not interact at all with the informants and they may not be aware that they are being observed.

Gold has noted that each of his four field

roles offers certain advantages and disadvantages to the researcher. However, the role of complete participant has been heavily criticised in the literature in terms of ethical implications and the limitations on data collection that it imposes (Caudill, 1958; Erikson, 1967).

PARTICIPANT OBSERVATION
PITFALL # 1

IT'S MY TRAIN—GET YOUR OWN!

GETTING TOO INVOLVED

Overall, the data collected by means of participant observation is considered to be rich and comprehensive in nature. It is also relatively open ended and unstructured. The initial purpose of the observations is to gain as complete an understanding as possible of the situation under study. Having obtained an overall view of the situation, the researcher might narrow the focus of the observations to a more specific field of interest.

Data Collection
From a natural science perspective, a researcher would solve the problem of what data to collect by operationalising the concepts as fully as possible. That is, categories of behaviour would be identified and carefully defined and coding schemes developed to facilitate data collection, with these tasks being completed for the most part from the perspective of the researcher. In contrast, the participant observer would, in most instances, attempt as much as possible to avoid developing pre-determined categories arising out

of the researcher's own perceptions of the
situation. Instead, by spending as much time as
possible in the situation, participating in the
activities, interviewing and talking with people
and carefully observing, the means for describing
the scene or situation should emerge out of the
informant's own "lived experience". That is, the
informant's own constructs would serve to
structure the research.

An excellent example of this approach to data
collection is found in Sherry Pittman's (1985)
study of teacher's management strategies. Her
data was collected over a 15 month period and
involved 23 hours of interviewing and 30 hours of
observation every two weeks. Having gained an
overall understanding of the school day, her focus
narrowed to a study of teacher-student interaction
and more particularly on the classroom management
of students engaged in the on-task behaviour of
reading. Observation and interview produced
hypotheses about teacher behaviour that were
tested against observed behaviour. This procedure
facilitated the development of teacher's
rationales for classroom management.

Methods for Recording Participant Observations
"Once in the field, the participant observer is
typically somewhat overwhelmed by data, the
meaning of which is not always immediately
apparent and therefore must be mulled over"
(Strauss, Schatzman, Bucher, Ehrlich, & Sabshin,
1964, p.28). As Strauss et al go on to note, it
is impossible to record everything, but as a
general rule it is a good principle to record more
detail than what is thought to be needed.

The actual methods used to record behaviour
vary a great deal. Mehan (1979) has argued for
the use of observational techniques that record as
much as possible and preserve to the greatest
extent, the raw data. However, in order to best
elicit the meaning of the observations, it is
critical to record as fully as possible the
context in which the observations are made and the
behaviours occur. Presently, there is an
increasing use of video and audio-recorders in
participant observation (Collier, 1973; Mehan,
1979). It is important to note that the use of a
video-recorder does not guarantee that the context
is recorded. The researcher may need to
supplement direct recordings with written notes.
The advantages and disadvantages of mechanical

aids for recording data are outlined later in Chapter 6.

Data Retrieval

Of course, having recorded the observations, the researcher is still faced with the problem of retrieving and interpreting the data. Efforts to categorise behaviours range from the matrices developed by Flanders (1970) to the categories developed by Pittman (1985). Certainly, modern computer technology provides a way of coping with the large amounts of data collected over months or years of observation. To date though, the application of computer technology to participant observation is largely an undeveloped field. As such, participant observers typically rely on hand-written collation and indexing of raw data.

Whyte (1960) has developed one means for retrieving data from observations. His system involves dividing a page into three columns for each observation. The columns are headed (i) the number of the observation and date of data collection (ii) the people observed and (iii) the relevant topics and verbal and non-verbal behaviour observed. Whyte recommends that the construction of categories of behaviour be delayed until 8 or 10 observations have been made and some sense of the situation has been obtained. At that point, the researcher can re-read notes, and develop appropriate categories. This procedure is repeated periodically as further observations are made. Here it is worthwhile repeating that the categories developed for coding the observations should arise out of the informant's own lived experience in order that they reflect theirs and not the researcher's ideas.

Reliability and Validity of Observations Made Using Participant Observation

In a seminal paper on the issue of reliability and validity of observation in participant observation Lecompte and Goetz (1982, p.31) note:

> The value of scientific research is partially dependent on the ability of individual researchers to demonstrate the credibility of their findings. Regardless of the discipline or the methods used for data collection and analysis all scientific ways of knowing strive for authentic results. In all fields that engage in scientific enquiry reliability and

validity of findings are important.

The apparent lack of standardised procedures for conducting participant observation and issues such as lack of separation between observer and observed has led many scientists to be unconvinced of the quality of the data and of the conclusions generated by the method. Doubts have been expressed about whether two researchers using participant observation can arrive at comparable results. Other doubts have been expressed about whether data obtained in one study at one point is replicable in another study at another point. Still further questions have been raised about whether data obtained from participant observations are valid indicators of underlying phenomenon. Such questions are deserving of the fullest consideration, but until recently have not been addressed in the most complete manner by researchers using participant observation.

As already noted, a searching examination of the issues of reliability and validity in relation to qualitative research has been conducted by Lecompte and Goetz (1982). They have drawn attention to the distinctive characteristics of qualitative as opposed to quantitative research traditions and argued that these characteristics result in variations in the ways the problems of reliability and validity are approached. However, they argue that given the common description of reliability as a concern with replicability of scientific findings, various strategies are available to qualitative researchers to enhance the reliability of their results. Thus, qualitative researchers can enhance reliability by clearly identifying methods of data collection and analysis, distinguishing between observations requiring low and high inference by the researcher, using multiple researchers who are highly trained and employing technology such as video-tape to record their data. Given that validity of scientific findings refers to their accuracy both Lecompte and Goetz (1982) and Pittman (1985) have argued that the validity of qualitative research methods can be enhanced by the strategy of alternating between direct observation and systematic indirect questioning to discover the logically related principles used by individuals and groups to order relevant phenomenon.

In summary, writers are now giving serious

consideration to the vexatious questions of reliability and validity of data in qualitative research. Investigators are now being asked to seriously consider these issues in order to enhance the credibility of their findings.

EXAMPLES OF DIRECT OBSERVATION IN HERMENEUTIC RESEARCH

The following examples of research provide some insight into how investigators have used direct observation techniques within an hermeneutic tradition. Burnett (1967) used an ethnographic approach in her study of how differences between household cultures and school culture in an urban Puerto Rican community in Chicago affect children's behaviour in school. As part of her research she investigated how Puerto Rican notions of "machismo" influenced the interaction of male students with female teachers.

Her methodology involved extensive interviews and observations enabling her to gather information on how students and adults viewed each other and their common problems. Burnett developed the means for comparing "observed events" in the classroom and community setting. Her observations involved describing events in terms of their location in space and time, the people present, their actions and interactions, both verbal and non-verbal, and the order in which the various events occurred.

In another study Carraher, Carraher and Schliemann (1985) used a method that they described as a hybrid between the Piagetian clinical method and participant observation in their study of the everyday use of mathematics by Brazilian children in commercial transactions, e.g., children selling vegetables. The researchers had hypothesised that there might be differences in the way children solved problems as taught in schools and the way they solved problems in familiar working contexts, e.g., street corners outside of school hours. From their findings they concluded that mathematics might be best taught by providing real life examples for children to solve because it appeared that problem solving was more often found in the context of real life settings, e.g., children working out the cost of selling fruit than in classroom settings. From a methodological point of view Carraher et al (1985, p.27) noted that "... the combination of the clinical method of questioning with participant observation used in this project seemed particularly helpful when exploring mathematical thinking and thinking in daily life".

CHAPTER SUMMARY
Direct observation is an important facet of the research endeavour in the new hermeneutic. As illustrated in this chapter though, the nature of the observations made within this line of research differs in intent and purpose from the observations made within a more quantitative research framework. Perhaps the most significant difference is that within an hermeneutic tradition the observations are more keenly directed towards providing insight into the "inner" (subject's) world and its meanings for him or her, as opposed to the observer's constructed view of the world. This important difference influences how the observations are collected, recorded and interpreted. It also poses problems in relation to the issue of the reliability and validity of the findings although as argued in this chapter these problems are by no means insurmountable.

Chapter Six

RECORDING BEHAVIOUR

I learned this at least, by my experiment: that if one advances confidently in the direction of his dreams, and endeavours to live the life which he has imagined, he will meet with a success unexpected in common hours.

(Thoreau, 1960, p.215)

INTRODUCTION

Strategies for recording the stream of behaviour have undergone considerable change in the brief history of child study. Currently, in choosing a recording method, a child observer is presented with a number of options ranging from narrative diary descriptions, checklists, voice recorders, event recorders and video-recorders. The methods differ from each other in terms of cost, complexity, ease of use and type of data provided for analysis. These are a few of the considerations that must be weighed up by the investigator in choosing a particular method.

In the present chapter, attention is given to describing a number of the more commonly used methods for recording behaviour and outlining their associated advantages and disadvantages. The methods discussed include:

1. checklists
2. tape recorders
3. event recorders
4. video-tape recorders.

Checklists

The checklist is an observation instrument that has been used extensively by scientists involved in animal studies and also by psychologists interested in the study of human behaviour.

Recording Behaviour

The checklist is usually a sheet prepared for data collection before the actual observations begin. The usual form is composed of columns for categories of behaviour, e.g., looking or vocalizing and rows for units of time (see Table 6.1). The observer simply places a check in the row corresponding to the behaviours as they occur. The behaviours are coded in successive columns as the time blocks elapse and a given behaviour is entered only once every time block. Checklists are often used in conjunction with some time sampling method (e.g., one-zero). For example, the researcher may observe for one minute and take ten seconds out to record the behaviours on the checklist. Generally, the observer is fitted with an earplug to provide a sensory cue to indicate the end of each time interval.

An example of a checklist is provided in Table 6.1. The mother's and infant's behaviour during play is being recorded at 30 second intervals with a 5 second break between intervals to record behaviour. The behaviours coded include, (i) maternal vocalization, (ii) infant vocalization, (iii) mother looks at infant, and (iv) infant looks at mother.

Table 6.1. Checklist for Recording Mother-Infant Interaction

Time	Maternal Voc	Infant Voc	Mother looks at Infant	Infant looks at Mother
00	X		X	X
30		X		
60				
90				X
120				

Advantages of Checklists

Checklists have an extensive history as a recording device. They have the advantage of being relatively inexpensive, easy to construct and provide immediate access to the data without need for electronic intervention.

Disadvantages of Checklists

1. Perhaps the principle disadvantage of checklists is that they limit the number of behaviours that can be recorded at any one time.

2. It is also often difficult to obtain a high level of reliability with checklists because the observer has to look away to record.

3. Another problem is that the stream of behaviour is broken when time-out is taken to record behaviour. As such, unless specifically developed, the sequential nature of behaviour is often difficult to determine from checklists.

Summary

Checklists have been used extensively in child observation studies. For the interested reader excellent reviews of this method of recording behaviour are provided by Brandt (1972) and Hinde (1973).

Tape Recorders

Tape recording a voice narrative of ongoing behaviour is another method for collecting observations. Usually tape recording does not involve a classification of anticipated behaviours before making the observations but the researcher describes the flow of behaviour as it unfolds for later analysis. Having recorded the data the next step is to prepare a transcript and then identify selected behaviours from the transcript. The tape recorder is also useful for obtaining a relatively permanent record of interviews with subjects which are subsequently transcribed and analysed. Russell (1980) has used this method in a study of maternal perceptions of infant behaviour.

Advantages of Tape Recordings

1. Recording a commentary onto tape is far quicker than making written notes and need not involve the observer in breaking

the stream of behaviour to record the observations.
2. The method is relatively inexpensive.
3. The small amount of equipment involved allows the observer freedom to move about and follow the subject. For example, in studying children's playground behaviour a tape recorder would allow an observer to freely follow children in the playground and would be a relatively unobtrusive method.

Disadvantages of Tape Recordings
1. Whilst the time spent recording observations may be minimal the transcription of the tapes can be very time-consuming.
2. Another problem includes that of obtaining an adequate level of observer reliability. The use of a two channel tape recorder permits the simultaneous recording of observations on a child by two observers which can be used to assess inter-rater reliability. A problem associated with that of reliability is that the interpretation of the data depends on what the observer chooses to record or describe.

Summary
Tape recordings have not been extensively used in the field of child study. Smith and Connolly (1972) have used the method in the study of free-play behaviour in pre-school children and their research may provide the reader with some idea of the strengths and weaknesses of the approach.

Event Recorders
In the last decade, event recorders have come to be widely used in child observation studies (Fogel, 1977; Stephenson, 1979). In event recorders ink or heat stylus pens are connected to buttons on a control board. Each button corresponds to a discrete behaviour and when the button is pressed the corresponding pen is displaced leaving a record on a strip chart which is moving at a calibrated speed to provide a time base. The behaviour is summarised by measuring the length of each deflection and converting the

length to time units. The frequency, duration and sequence of behaviours· are then coded onto a summary sheet. Usually the number of behavioural categories that can be recorded is limited to the number of pens on the recorder.

Advantages of Event Recorders
Perhaps the primary advantage of event recorders is that they provide a measure of the frequency, duration and sequencing of behaviours as they occur in "real time". That is, unlike checklists where the time units are imposed on the behaviour stream and the behaviour recorded only once per time interval regardless of how many times it has occurred, the event recorder measures every occurrence of a particular behaviour.

Disadvantages of Event Recorders
1. Event recorders are quite labour intensive in nature, costly, and often limit the number of behaviours that can be recorded. To overcome the labour intensive problem, researchers have adapted the method for use with computers. For example, Anderson and Vietze (1977) used an event recorder in a study of mother-infant vocal dialogue in the natural home setting. The system consists of a hand-held numeric keyboard connected to a cassette tape recorder strapped over the shoulder. The observer presses keyboard buttons representing digits 0-9, to generate a signal which is silently recorded on a cassette tape. The cassette tape can be inter-faced with a computer magnetic tape system to facilitate data analysis. Similarly, Simpson (1979) has developed a 40 channel event recorder which is computer compatible.

2. Perhaps the most serious limitation of event recorders is that they impose an "on-off" quality on the recorded behaviour. As such, the method is best used where the behaviours under observation have a clear beginning and end, e.g., vocalization or gaze. Behaviours which start gradually or taper off, e.g., "affectionate" or "warm" emotional expression would be very difficult to record using a keyboard

system (Slee, 1982). The event recorder also lacks flexibility if the investigator is interested in reviewing the behavioural sequence several times.

Summary
Event recorders have considerable application in the field of child study but as with any method the investigator must weigh up their associated advantages and disadvantages. For further information on this recording method the reader is referred to Simpson (1979) and Stephenson (1979).

Video-Tape Recorders
In the last decade, video-tape recording has enjoyed considerable popularity as a method of child study. As Eisler, Hersen and Agras (1973, p.420) have noted:

> The facility of modern video-tape equipment to record and store massive amounts of complex behavioural information with the capacity for an indefinite number of relatively instantaneous replays would appear to make it an invaluable research tool in the study of human interactive behaviour.

Research indicates that assessment of interpersonal behaviour can be made as reliably from video-tapes as from live observations (Eisler et al, 1973). Video-tape recordings lend themselves to a range of child study situations including laboratory settings (Brazelton, Koslowski & Main, 1974) and natural home settings (Russell, 1983).

Typically, recording facilities involve two cameras, video-recorder, special effects generator and a television monitor. Input from the two cameras is fed into a special effects generator which is used to edit the input from the cameras and produce a composite picture.

Advantages of Video-Tape Recording
1. An important advantage of the method includes the facility it offers for multiple viewings. Researchers such as Heidelise, Tronick and Brazelton (1979, p.36) have chosen video-tape as their recording method "since it makes the

sequence immediately and repeatedly available for playback".

2. Another advantage of the method is that it provides a relatively permanent and complete verbal and non-verbal record of the behaviours.

3. A video-recording also goes some way towards preserving the context in which the observations are made.

Disadvantages of Video-Tape Recording

1. A significant disadvantage of the method which often prohibits its use includes the high cost of the equipment.

2. There are also technical limitations associated with the camera's restricted field of view and the problem that the resolution of detail is inversely proportional to the field of view of the cameras.

3. Video-recording also induces a good deal of self consciousness in subjects during observation which may markedly affect their behaviour.

4. The method can also be quite labour intensive requiring as it may do, a number of personnel to record the observations (Slee, 1982).

Summary

Overall, in recent years the method of video-taping in child study has enjoyed considerable popularity. As Newson (1977, p.51) has noted in a study of mother-infant interaction:

> The problem for the observer is the extraordinary speed with which signals are typically exchanged, so that even with very young infants it seems essential to capture the communication sequence on film or video allowing the observer to review them repeatedly in context and from the standpoint of each of the participants independently.

CHAPTER SUMMARY

In this chapter, a number of the more commonly used methods for recording behaviour in child study have been described along with their associated advantages and disadvantages. Points to consider in choosing a recording method include:

- the nature of the behaviours under study, e.g., a tape recorder might be chosen if the study involved only verbal behaviour
- the number of behaviours under study, e.g., a video-recorder might be used if a range of verbal and non-verbal behaviours were being studied
- consideration of the situation in which the study is to be made, e.g., in a playground study of children's social behaviour the considerable mobility required to follow children around might preclude the use of bulky video-recorders
- the cost of the equipment and the number of personnel involved.

Chapter Seven

OBSERVATION SCHEMES

I sought no more that, after which I strayed,
In face of man or maid:
But still within the little children's eyes
Seems something, something that replies,
They at least are for me, surely for me!
I turned me to them very wistfully;
But just as their young eyes grew sudden fair
With dawning answers there
Their angel plucked them from me by the hair.

(F. Thompson, 1947)

INTRODUCTION

Having chosen an appropriate research design
(Chapter 3), considered the method for sampling
the stream of behaviour (Chapter 5) and identified
the best means for recording the observations
(Chapter 6), the researcher is in a position to
choose or develop an observation scheme. A brief
survey of recent developmental psychology
literature by the interested reader will reveal a
plethora of child observation schemes developed by
researchers. The historical antecedents of these
observational schemes are to be found in the diary
notations of scientifically minded parents. For
example, Charles Darwin used diary observations of
his own children in the development of his theory
of the expression of emotions in humans. Thus, in
describing the emotion of anger he notes: "With
one of my own infants under four months old, I
repeatedly observed that the first symptom of an
approaching passion was the rushing of blood into
his bare scalp." (Darwin, 1965, p.238).

Early this century, observers developed time
sampling and event sampling techniques in an
effort to further quantify their observations.
With the advent of checksheets, mechanical

recording devices (e.g., video-tape) and more recently computers, the nature of observational schemes used in child study has undergone considerable change. In developing an observation scheme, researchers are confronted with a number of issues and decisions that will influence the nature and effectiveness of the scheme including:
1. the nature of behaviour to be observed,
2. the task of developing a coding scheme,
3. the advantages of adapting an existing scheme,
4. the need to gather more than observational data to explain phenomena,
A list of coding schemes used in child study available to teachers, psychologists and social workers is presented in the Appendix.

THE NATURE OF BEHAVIOUR
Observing and interpreting behaviour is part of the commerce of our everyday interactions with others. As Mayo and La France (1978, p.217) note, "Becoming communicative involves attending to others, responding to them, and knowing how one's own responses affect others in turn." Those interested in child behaviour are concerned with the process of describing behaviour and finding in it some order and predictability. However, in developing a coding scheme, the temptation is to overlook the assumptions, implicit or explicit, we make, when we take behaviour and interrupt its flow, categorize it and de-contextualize it. As such, consideration needs to be given to some of the inherent properties of behaviour prior to the development of a coding scheme including: (i) the molar versus molecular nature of behaviour, (ii) levels of behaviour, (iii) frequency, intensity, duration and sequencing of behaviour, and (iv) behaviour observation versus rating scales for recording behaviour.

The Molar vs Molecular Nature of Behaviour
The terms molar and molecular refer to the breadth of behaviour. For example, one might be interested in recording a spectogram of a baby's cries or analysing frame-by-frame movements of a baby's facial expressions during play interaction with its mother. Stern, Jaffe, Beebe, and Bennett (1975) used a frame-by-frame film analysis of mother-infant interaction in their study of vocal behaviour during play interaction. Such fine-grained molecular analysis of behaviour would

contrast with a broader molar analysis of the content of a mother's speech to her child. For example, Slee (1983,b) examined the content of mothers' vocal utterances over 5 second periods in a study of mother-infant emotional behaviour. It would be a mistake to view a molar and molecular approach to the study of behaviour as incompatible because the two can be combined. However, it should be recognized that behaviour can be viewed in these terms and the approach adopted to the coding of behaviour will depend on the purpose of the study and the questions being asked.

Levels of Behaviour

A somewhat overlapping consideration to that of molar vs molecular behaviour in developing a coding scheme concerns the issue of the level of behaviour coded. Yarrow and Waxler (1979, p.44) advocate that "...observers might explicitly sort out different levels of behaviour: crisp physical detail of space and motion; low level psychological inference; alternative conceptual frameworks, a referencing of behaviour to its contexts, and so on". That is, they argue that it is necessary to recognize and allow for the fundamental complexity of behaviour in developing a coding scheme.

An illustration of the different levels of behaviour utilized in a coding scheme is provided in a study by Jones (1980). He notes that in order to understand the nature of mother-infant gaze behaviour it may be necessary to move beyond the simple coding of whether or not the individuals involved are looking at each other. Jones has classified eye-contact into three major types; (a) personal, where social contact is made, (b) game, where gaze serves a role in games between mother and child, and (c) referential, where eye contact provides information about an event outside the dyad, e.g., the infant signals that she wants a toy.

In developing a coding scheme then, an observer might incorporate different levels of behaviour in the scheme. In determining the nature of the scheme "the goal is for the appropriate match of measure and research question" (Yarrow & Waxler, 1979, p.45).

Observation Schemes

Frequency, Intensity, Duration and Sequencing of Behaviour

The attributes of frequency, intensity, duration and sequencing of behaviour warrant important consideration in developing a coding scheme. Their use and incorporation in a scheme will depend in large part on the purpose of the study and the nature of the questions being asked of the data.

Frequency. In obtaining a measure of the frequency of a behaviour an observer will be concerned with how often the behaviour occurs. As noted in Chapter 4, the accuracy with which frequency measures are obtained will depend upon how the behaviour stream is sampled (event vs time sampling) and the nature of the behaviour itself (discrete vs ill-defined behaviour).

Intensity. This refers to the strength of a behaviour. It is a measure that is not used a great deal in observational studies because it is difficult to judge reliably the intensity with which a behaviour occurs. However, researchers such as Gaensbauer, Mrazek and Emde (1979) and Kogan and Gordon (1975) have used intensity measures to assess emotional expression in mothers and children.

Duration. This aspect of behaviour refers to how long it persists. For example, researchers have studied gaze length in mother-infant interaction (Stern, 1974). Similarly, Liebert and Baron (1972) clocked the duration of each aggressive response in their observation of school children who had watched either aggressive or non-aggressive television shows. They found that the average duration of aggressive responses was longer among children who had watched the aggressive shows, while the absolute frequencies with which the behaviours occurred did not differ among the programmes. As such, the nature of the behaviour recorded was an important discriminating factor in their study.

Sequencing. The reference here is to the analysis of events following each other. For example, Lytton and Zwirner (1975) studied the effect of parents' verbal behaviour upon the compliance of their children to their verbal statements. Researchers have observed mother and infant gaze

(Stern, 1974; Slee, 1984) and vocalization patterns (Schaffer, Collis & Parsons, 1977). In these studies, the interaction between the participants has been represented as a sequence of discrete states. That is, at each successive time interval individuals might be (a) active, (b) quiescent, (c) the mother is active and the infant is inactive, or (d) the infant is active and the mother is inactive. From this sequential data it is possible to obtain information on the likelihood of one state following another. For example, using sequential analysis, it has been found that during the first year of life mother-infant vocal interaction approximates an adult "dialogue-like" nature (Slee, 1983,b).

There has been a renewed interest in the sequential analysis of observational data in the last decade. For further information the interested reader is referred to Gottman and Bakeman (1979), and Castellan (1979).

Behaviour Observation vs Rating Scales for Recording Behaviour.

The relative merits of behaviour observations and rating scales for recording behaviour have been the subject of considerable and at times, heated, debate in psychology. In Chapter 4, consideration was given to the advantages and disadvantages of rating scales. The identifying feature of rating scales is that they involve judgements by an observer of the placement of an individual on some psychological dimension. For example, Ainsworth (1971) used a 9 point scale to rate mothers for

(i)   sensitivity-insensitivity,
(ii)   acceptance-rejection,
(iii)   co-operation-interference, and
(iv)   accessibility-ignoring

during interaction with their child.

As Cairns and Green (1979) note, rating scales rely heavily on the capability of the rater. They identify the following assumptions made about the capabilities of raters:

1. the raters have the same understanding of the behaviours which best reflect the behaviour being rated,

2. the raters have the same understanding of the underlying theory of the quality being rated,

3. the rater has the ability to abstract information about whether or not particular acts occurred and interpret the causes and meanings of the acts,

4. the rater shares along with others the same underlying scale on which the quality will be judged.

In examining these assumptions, it is not difficult to see why rating is considered by researchers to be a very difficult task. However, for some research problems, ratings are the most appropriate methods to use. For example, ratings are more useful for assessing the stability of behaviour and for identifying characteristic features or styles of an individual's behaviour.

For those investigators who aspire to describe individual differences in behavioural style, or distinctive properties of an interaction between two or more persons, ratings can be most useful. They help clarify the everyday judgements each of us makes about other persons in classifying them, their behaviour and their relationships (Cairns & Green, 1979, p.223).

Using behaviour observations, the focus is very much on the precise actions of individuals. The nature of behavioural observations is well described by Sackett (1978, p.25) who notes:

the observed individual emits motor and verbal responses, in various sequences, lasting for variable durations. The observer employs arbitrary codes identifying these responses, attempting to measure exactly how the observed person fills time. This is done by either scoring the onset or offset of codable behaviour, or scoring the presence of codable behaviours at specific time sampling intervals.

The role of the observer is to record behaviour. As such it is important that the behaviours to be recorded are clearly defined and identified and that the observers have the ability to record the selected behaviours. It should be borne in mind that behavioural observations and rating scales are not two mutually exclusive methods and that it is possible to combine them in a coding scheme (Kogan & Gordon, 1975; Slee, 1983,b, 1984).

Summary
Properties of behaviour are of critical importance
in developing a coding scheme. By its very nature
behaviour is part of an ongoing stream, making
identification of parts of the stream a difficult
process. It is important to recognize that in
breaking into this stream the observer is making
decisions about the molar or molecular state of
behaviour, the level at which the behaviour is
studied, the quality of behaviour and the way the
behaviour will be recorded. All of these
decisions will influence the nature of the coding
scheme developed, the nature of the data available
for analysis and ultimately the nature of the
questions that can be asked of the data. As such,
considerable thought needs to be given to these
questions in developing a coding scheme. As
Yarrow and Waxler (1979, p.38) note, "When the
results of research are truly elegant and stable,
one can be quite certain not only that the
research question was meaningful but also that the
methods by which the data was derived had a worthy
level of precision or sensitivity".

THE TASK OF DEVELOPING A CODING SCHEME
The complex problem of developing a coding scheme
requires a number of important decisions by the
researcher. Consideration will now be given to
the nature of these decisions. Emphasis will be
given to: (1) choosing a category as opposed to a
sign system, (2) sampling the stream of behaviour,
(3) choosing a recording method, (4) the
observer's role in the observational process, and
(5) assessing the reliability of the scheme.

1. Category vs Sign System
Medley and Mitzel (1963) have identified two broad
approaches to the development of coding schemes,
namely category and sign systems. The rationale
behind a category system is that the coding scheme
provides a set of behaviours, which are intended
to be relatively exhaustive of all the behaviours
likely to occur in the situation being studied.
For example, Kogan, Wimberger and Bobbitt (1969)
developed a coding system constituting some 43
categories intended to describe mother-infant
interaction in terms of spatial position, posture,
locomotion, visual contact, manipulation, and
expressive-gestural behaviour.

A coding scheme utilizing a sign system involves a more limited set of behaviours. For example, Stern (1977) limited his coding of mother-infant interaction to gaze behaviour.

In developing a coding scheme a researcher must give some consideration to whether a category or sign system will be employed. In turn, this decision will depend in large part on the purpose of the scheme and the research questions or hypotheses being addressed.

2. Sampling the Stream of Behaviour

Sampling the stream of behaviour requires careful consideration. Sampling procedures may be considered as either (i) time independent or (ii) time dependent. A time independent method (event sampling) involves identifying particular events, e.g., aggression and recording the event when and if it occurs. Time dependent measures involve dividing the behaviour stream into time intervals (e.g., 5 second period) with each interval being scored for the presence or absence of behaviour.

In Chapter 4 full consideration was given to the advantages and disadvantages of time independent and time dependent measures for sampling the stream of behaviour. In devising a coding scheme, the researcher's decision concerning which method to use is influenced by factors such as the method by which the behaviour was recorded, the nature of the behaviour under observation and the type of analyses to be performed on the data. For example, as a general rule, infrequently occurring behaviours (temper tantrums) are best recorded using an event sampling method.

3. Choosing a Recording Method

In Chapter 6 various methods for collecting data were described including the use of checklists, event recorders, voice recorders, and video-tape recorders. Each method has its advantages and disadvantages. Factors influencing which method is used include the capital cost of the equipment, the type of data being collected and the research questions being answered.

4. The Observer's Role in the Observational Process

The role the observer plays while recording the observations needs careful thought given that the observer's presence will influence the subject's behaviour. In mainstream psychological research, every effort is usually made to minimize the effect of the observer on the subject's behaviour. Johnson and Bolstadt (1973) have identified four sources of reactivity to an observer's presence including (i) the conspicuousness of the observer, (ii) individual differences in subjects to being observed, (iii) personal attributes of the observer, and (iv) whether or not a rationale is provided for the observations.

(i)   Conspicuousness of the observer: There is evidence to suggest that the presence of an observer increases the rate of positive and desirable behaviours in subjects. For example, Zegiob and Forehand (1975) found that mothers were more verbally positive, played with their infants more and structured their children's activities more when they were aware of the observer's presence than when they were not. Some thought should be given then to minimizing the conspicuousness of the observer where possible. Techniques that have been tried include self recording, minimizing the amount of equipment used, e.g., checksheets instead of video-recorders, or using familiarization visits prior to commencing observations. It is very difficult to assess how far such techniques go toward reducing subject's reactivity to observation but some thought should be given to incorporating one or more of the methods in the design of the observation procedure.

(ii)   Individual differences in subjects to being observed: It has been noted that young children are less self-conscious than older children during observation. This factor might be taken into account when observing children.

(iii)   Personal attributes of the observer: The observer's age, sex and professional status have been associated with subject's reactivity to observation (Martin, Gelfand & Hartman, 1971). The self-consciousness in subjects generally relates to feelings of being "judged" or "evaluated". One method for offsetting such feelings is to avoid being cast in the role of an "expert".

For example, observers might be instructed not to talk to mothers about their child-rearing techniques or problems they are experiencing with their children.

(iv) Providing a rationale for the study: To minimize anxiety and guardedness about being observed one strategy is to explain the purpose of the study as fully as possible to the subjects. Of course, care must be taken to do this without unduly influencing the outcome of the study. The rationale is that explaining the purpose of the study to the subject will minimize their need to imagine why they are being observed or why they have been chosen.

In summary, consideration should be given to the role the observer will play in the observation process because of the effect of the observer on the subject's behaviour. Methods for minimizing reactivity to observation vary from rendering the observer as inconspicuous as possible, the "fly on the wall" approach, to participant observation where the observations are carried out while the observer participates as naturally as possible with the subjects. Whatever approach is adopted along this continuum, at the very least, "investigators have to accept the behaviour seen as behaviour-in-the-presence-of-an-observer" (Lytton, 1980, p.35).

5. Reliability

In the course of developing the coding scheme attention must be given to estimating its reliability. "A demonstration of high reliability is critical to conclude that a strong relationship exists between the behaviour emitted by the subjects and the behaviour recorded by the observer" (Lipinski & Nelson, 1974, p.33). In the literature, reference is typically made to two types of reliability, namely, inter-rater and intra-rater reliability. Inter-rater reliability refers to the level of agreement between two independent observers who have observed the same situation and then compared the level of agreement in their observations. Intra-rater reliability refers to a single observer's level of agreement on a number of observations made over a period of time. It is a necessary measure to employ to check the level of "observer drift" or the tendency in coding observations for accuracy to decline over time. It is usually calculated by making spot checks of the observations in the course of the study.

The level of reliability is usually expressed as a correlation. Perfect agreement between two measures is expressed as a correlation of +1.00. When there is no agreement the correlation is 0. A negative correlation (e.g., -1.00) indicates that when one factor is present the other is missing. One of the most commonly used formulas for estimating reliability is:

$$\text{reliability} = \frac{\text{no. of agreements (of two observers)}}{\text{no. of agreements} + \text{no. of disagreements}} \times 100$$

For example, in estimating the inter-rater reliability of the coding of infant vocalization using a time sampling procedure, the method would involve having two observers record infant vocalization over a period of time. The data might appear as follows:

5 second interval	Observer 1	Observer 2
5	✓	✓
10	✓	✓
15	✓	✓
20	✓	
25	✓	

Applying the above formula inter-rater reliability = $\dfrac{3}{3 + 2}$ x 100

$$= 3/5 \times 100$$

$$= .60 \text{ (or 60\%)}$$

There is no minimum level of reliability for a coding scheme although from the literature, consensus suggests that a level of .80 is acceptable. Overall then, in developing a coding scheme it is important to assess both inter- and intra-rater reliability.

PUTTING THE SCHEME TOGETHER
As outlined in this chapter, the task of developing a coding scheme is quite complex with the researcher making a number of important decisions at various stages in the process. In constructing a scheme, the following steps might be followed, keeping in mind that they are not necessarily sequential, and on occasions several might be completed simultaneously,

1.   Become familiar with the subjects and the situation in which the observations are to be made. This might be done by means of preliminary casual observations, by talking to other people who have been

      involved in similar studies and by reviewing the literature.

2. Begin keeping a record of preliminary observations perhaps via narrative description or tape recorder. Start focussing more narrowly on the behaviours that can be observed and thinking about the best means for recording the behaviours.

3. Clarify the questions to be asked or the hypotheses to be tested. This process will help identify the behaviours to be studied and provide insight into the best way to record the behaviours. A careful review of the literature will identify previous studies that have been made in the area under consideration and may unearth coding schemes that have already been developed.

4. Using a pilot coding scheme attempt to record selected behaviours, taking into account whether behaviour observations or rating scales are to be used.

5. Experiment with various methods for recording behaviour e.g., check lists, or tape recorders.

6. Revise the pilot coding scheme and test it under actual observation conditions. Assess inter-rater reliability. Some guidelines for the selection of categories in a coding scheme include:
   (i) Comprehensiveness - this refers to how adequately the categories capture the intent of the observations.
   (ii) Relevance - are the categories relevant to the questions or hypotheses under study?

7. Carefully consider the nature of the data generated by the coding scheme and the type of statistical analyses to be performed on the data. Consider whether the data generated and analysed will answer the questions or hypotheses under study.

The guidelines provided here are not prescriptive. There are few hard and fast rules for developing a coding scheme. Some flavour of the process involved in developing a coding scheme is found in the sentiment expressed by Margret Bullowa (1975, p.126):

When we who work with film and video present "data", we do not usually tell of the hours of struggle we have gone through before finding some order in the passing scene. Once we find it, there is a Eureka feeling and it all seems so self evident.

An alternative to developing one's own coding scheme is to adapt an existing scheme to the needs and purposes of one's study.

ADAPTING AN EXISTING SCHEME
As noted at the beginning of the present chapter there are currently a large number of coding schemes available to teachers, psychologists and child-care workers. A brief listing and commentary on a selected number of published schemes is presented in the Appendix. On occasion it is appropriate to extend or adapt an existing scheme to meet the specific needs of a study.

For example, The Flanders Interaction Analysis Scheme has been adapted by various researchers. As defined by Flanders (1970, p.5) interaction analysis is "... a label that refers to any technique for studying the chain of classroom events in such a fashion that each event is taken into consideration". Flanders was particularly interested in teacher-student verbal interaction. His coding scheme includes seven teacher-talk categories, two pupil-talk categories and one category to indicate silence or confusion. Details of the scheme are provided in Table 7.1.

Table 7.1: Flanders Interaction Analysis Code (FIAC)(1970)

Teacher Talk
Response
1. Accepts feelings of students in non threatening manner
2. Praises or encourages student
3. Accepts or uses ideas of students
4. Asks questions
Initiation
5. Lectures, gives facts or opinions
6. Gives directions
7. Criticises or justifies authority

Student Talk
Response
   8. Student talk in response to
      teacher
Initiation
   9. Student talk - initiated by
      students
  10. Silence or confusion

Then, using a tally sheet, an observer records one discrete category every three seconds. Flanders recommends that an observation session needs to last 20-25 minutes to obtain a sufficient number of observations for analysis. The FIAC is amenable to modification to suit a particular researcher's needs.

Bailey and Slee (1984) successfully adapted the scheme in a study of teachers' and parents' interaction with multiply handicapped children. Modification to a number of the individual categories of the FIAC is illustrated in Table 7.2.

Table 7.2: The Modified FIAC Scheme

Mother Talk
Response
   1. Accepts feelings of child in non
      threatening manner
   2. Praises or encourages the child
   3. Accepts or uses ideas of child
   4. Asks questions
Initiation
   5. Lectures, gives facts or opinions
   6. Gives directions
   7. Criticises or justifies authority
Child Talk
Response
   8. Child talk in response to mother
      - includes signing, i.e. manual
      communication, physical or oral
      communication
Initiation
   9. Child talk initiation expanded as
      in category 8
  10. Silence or confusion.

Using the specially modified FIAC, it was found that mothers of multiply disabled children exerted more direct influence during play interaction than mothers of normal children. Normal children were involved in more self-initiated communication than disabled children.

In adapting an existing scheme, considerable time is saved in developing coding categories and assessing reliability. However, care must be taken that the modified scheme will provide data that will answer the questions being asked in the study. Care must also be taken to test the reliability of the modified coding categories.

THE NEED FOR MORE THAN OBSERVATIONAL DATA

At this point, it is worthwhile commenting on some of the limitations of observational data for understanding behaviour. In Chapter 1, consideration was given to the manner in which the prevailing paradigm in psychology (positivism) emphasises the importance of overt action in explaining human behaviour. Recently, a number of authors have argued that more consideration should be given by researchers to other determinants of behaviour. As Russell (1980, p.19) notes, "...behaviourism has resulted in psychologists often ignoring or giving very little attention to what is seen as the main or actual determinants of human action, things such as the person's interpretations of the meaning of the situation, and other people's behaviour, the person's beliefs, goals, etc." Russell (1980) in a study involving 6 month old infants found evidence for reasonably direct links between maternal behaviour and underlying perceptions and beliefs. He found that maternal behaviours involved in the areas of "daily routines" and "attending to the baby when awake" could be reasonably explained in terms of a mixture of mothers' perceptions of infants and their needs and their beliefs about their roles as mothers.

In arguing for further research involving the relationship between cognitive factors and behaviour, Parke (1978) has argued that there is a need to "... distinguish between parental reports as objective measures of parental behaviour and parental reports as indices of parental knowledge, attitudes, stereotypes and perceptions. These latter classes of variables are legitimate and important sources of data and are not easily derived from observation alone". Parke believes that the latter type of data helps us understand how parents see, organize and understand their infants and their roles as parents and as such serve as filters through which the infants' behaviour is viewed.

It is worthwhile considering then, the possibility of supplementing observational data with other forms of data. As a caveat though, Russell (1980, p.23) has noted that "...the task of discovering the cognitive mediators of parent behaviour is one of enormous difficulty. It opens up issues and problems of research methodology that have so far been little explored in the literature on parent-child relations". For example, Russell raised the issue of whether cognitive mediators are to be restricted to beliefs or perceptions in conscious awareness or whether there are mediators that exist below or outside awareness. Another challenge that faces the researcher is to relate the various forms of data that are collected to make the most of the links among them.

CHAPTER SUMMARY
In this chapter, consideration has been given to better understanding the nature of behaviour and identifying some of its more characteristic features in relation to the task of developing a coding scheme. A number of guidelines were given as an aid to the researcher interested in developing a coding scheme. The point was made that on occasions it might be more appropriate to adapt an existing scheme. Finally, it was emphasised that sometimes observational data might need to be supplemented by other forms of data to more fully understand the phenomenon under investigation.

Chapter Eight

ASSESSING CHILDREN

Observational assessment is useful for
identifying children having emotional and/or
behavioural dis-orders, for making clinical
and education decisions regarding disturbed
children, and for measuring changes in
behaviour over time (Reed & Edelbrock, 1983,
p.521).

INTRODUCTION
Direct observation is an integral part of the
assessment of children's behaviour and is
routinely used by professionals working with
children such as teachers, social workers and
pyschologists. However, while direct observation
is the oldest and most common method for
understanding behaviour, its application in the
field of assessment has frequently lacked
direction and purpose. Problems associated with
the time and cost involved in observation work has
frequently meant that interview and questionnaire
data has taken precedence in the assessment
process. Recent advances in the methodology and
technology for observational work have offset some
of the disadvantages of the method. In this
chapter emphasis is given to:
. describing the vital role observation
plays in the assessment process in
educational and clinical settings
. describing for the practitioner, a sample
of observation schemes suitable for
application in school and clinical work
. outlining a flow chart whereby decisions
are made for using direct observation in
assessment
. evaluating the advantages and
disadvantages of direct observation in
assessment.

THE ASSESSMENT PROCESS

The following examples illustrate how a range of people working with children have recourse to direct observation for understanding their behaviour.

- In the middle of the school term, a new child is brought to the year 3 teacher's classroom. In the course of the following week the teacher observes the child to be withdrawn and depressed. The teacher notes that the child does not make friends easily and spends recess and lunch time alone. During class the child will often remark to the teacher "I love you Miss ..." where these comments are often out of context.

- A psychologist has a family referred to her for the assessment and treatment of their 3 year old child for anxiety and depression. During the initial interview it is noted that the child is warm, co-operative and friendly when the father, defacto wife and older sister are present. However, when the father leaves the room to take the older sister to the toilet, the child retreats away from the defacto wife to the furthest corner of the room and begins to whimper and cry.

- A social worker interviewing a father and young child in a custody case notes that the 4 year old boy spends most of the interview sitting on the floor holding and touching the worker's dress. The father is quite outspoken about his affection for the boy, but if he moves suddenly the child flinches and shifts closer to the social worker.

What do these three case studies share in common? In each instance there is observational data available to the professional working with the child. The challenge is to make maximum use of the data to assist in the assessment process. The basic question confronting the teacher or therapist is whether there is anything wrong with the child and it is to this question that consideration is now given.

Is Anything Wrong with the Child?

It is worth emphasising that just because a child is referred for therapy or comes to the notice of the classroom teacher does not mean that there is anything automatically wrong with the child. Thus, in the previous section the example of the child's behaviour in the new school may simply reflect some insecurity in adjusting to a new school regime. Further observations by the teacher over the following weeks might help answer whether or not the child's behaviour related primarily to settling into a new school.

There are also factors other than the child's problem behaviour that may bring them to the attention of professionals working with children. For example, Lobitz and Johnson (1975) identify marital distress, unrealistic parental expectations of children's behaviour, lack of parental knowledge about child development principles and low parental tolerance as contributing to referral to child guidance clinics. The first task in the assessment process then, involves determining whether or not there is anything wrong with the child. To this end there are a number of options open to those working with children outside of direct observation, including:

(i)   interviews with the referring adults
(ii)   having questionnaires on child behaviour completed by the referring adults
(iii)   interviews with the child.

(i) <u>Interviews with the Referring Adults</u>. Interviews with the child's parents or guardians are an important means for better understanding the child's behaviour. A free ranging interview provides the clinician/teacher with an invaluable opportunity for gathering information about the child and his family. Issues covered in the initial interview might include:

Why have the parents referred the child?
What are the particular problems which concern the parents?
When were the problems first noticed?
What makes the problems better or worse?
What impact are the problem(s) having on the life of the family?
What has been tried to solve the problem(s) and how has it worked?
Do you think other children of the child's age experience similar problems?
If appropriate, questions might be asked about the marital relationship, e.g., when and how the two met and married?

Information derived from the interview should clarify the nature of the parents' concerns about the child, their perception of the problem(s), their understanding of child development principles, whether or not the parents had previously sought help and from whom and what they would like done about the problem(s). Holland (1970) has developed a 21 step interview guide as an aid for conducting an assessment interview. Apart from the formal interviews, more informal contacts with parents (e.g., when picking their child up from school, assisting on an excursion or in the classroom) provide invaluable opportunities for gaining insight into the nature of the parent-child relationship and into the child's behaviour.

(ii) Questionnaires on Child Behaviour. Another method for gaining some insight into children's behaviour involves the use of questionnaires which are filled out by the child's parents or teachers (Slee, 1986). Questionnaires offer the clinician or teacher advantages in terms of ease of administration and scoring. Their primary disadvantage is that the data they provide is second-hand in nature. A brief review of the literature will identify a range of questionnaires that have been developed to assess various aspects of children's behaviour, e.g., temperament (Thomas, Chess & Birch, 1969).

(iii) Interviews with the Child. An interview with the child can provide the teacher or clinician with important insight into the presenting problem. Unfortunately, there are few guidelines available for interviewing children. Young children frequently find it threatening when faced with a therapist or teacher and may feel embarrassed, resentful or guilty at being confronted with their "problem" behaviour. To this end, an interview with a child may be approached indirectly through the medium of play (Gardner, 1975). Other activities such as drawing, or taking a walk with the child may help overcome anxiety or shyness. Therapeutic storytelling or sentence completion are other means for helping the child relax.

Summary
The task of judging whether or not a child really

has a problem is the first step in the assessment process. To this end, interviews with parents, questionnaires on child behaviour or interviews with the child are invaluable means for better understanding the validity of the problem. Apart from these indirect methods of gathering information direct observation of the child's behaviour is an invaluable means for gaining insight into the problem. The rest of this chapter is now given to describing how the teacher and clinician might use direct observation as a means for understanding the nature of children's behaviour.

OBSERVATION OF CHILDREN IN THE SCHOOL SETTING
Observation of children's behaviour is an everyday part of teaching activity. In the classroom, careful observations help the teacher in relation to learning goals, discipline, general classroom management and much more. More often than not the observations are made in a rather casual, unsystematic and unstructured fashion. Presently, there exists a range of research aimed at developing the means for observing children's behaviour in a more organised fashion. In Table 8.1 a selection of studies is provided illustrating the application of direct observation in school settings.

Table 8.1. Selected Studies of Direct Observation in School Settings

Study	Description of Children	Sampling Method	Behaviours Observed
Bryan, T.S. & Wheeler, R.L.D. (1972)	Normal children of kindergarten age	Bales Interaction Process Analysis	Task and non-task behaviour
Forness, S.R. & Esveldt, K. (1975)	Kindergarten children	One-zero time sampling	Verbal behaviour sampling
Beveridge, M. & Hurrell, P. (1979)	Handicapped children	Event sampling	Verbal and non-verbal behaviour
Scarlett, W.G. (1979)	Nursery school children	Continuous time sampling	Verbal and non-verbal behaviour

Table 8.1. (Cont'd.)

Field, T. (1980)	Kindergarten children	One-zero time sampling	Verbal and non-verbal behaviour
Novak, M., Olley, J.G. & Kearney, D. (1980)	Pre-school handi-capped and normal children	Continuous time sampling	Social play
Schumaker, J., Wildgen, J. & Sherman, J. (1982)	Children aged 12-1/2 to 16-1/2 years	Continuous time sampling	Social behaviour
Bailey, L. (1982)	Children aged 6-12 years	Continuous time sampling	Verbal behaviour
Reed, M. & Edelbrock, C. (1983)	Children aged 6-11 years	Narrative descrip-tion and rating scale	Verbal and non-verbal behaviour

For the most part, the studies outlined in Table 8.1. reflect the application of systematic classroom observation using pre-specified coding schemes. Such schemes reflect a positivist conception of research, the details of which were outlined in Chapter 1. In Table 8.1. the coding schemes may incorporate combinations of the following features:

Assessing Children
1. Category systems. Where every endeavour is made to code all of the individual's verbal and non-verbal behaviour, e.g., schemes which aim at classifying all possible types of questions asked by the teacher.
2. Sign systems. Where a limited range of teacher's or pupil's behaviour is focussed upon, e.g., coding a limited range of vocal behaviour such as "teacher talk".
3. Time dependent. Here the observation period is segmented into arbitrary time intervals and particular behaviours coded if they occur during an interval.

4. <u>Time independent</u>. Which includes systems that focus on particular events such as "in-seat" pupil behaviour and records such behaviour every time it occurs during the observation period.
5. <u>Highly inferential</u>. The observer is required to infer a good deal about the occurrence of a behaviour, e.g., teacher expressions of "warmth".
6. <u>Low in inference</u>. Here the behaviours are clearly specifiable, e.g., pupil vocalizes.

THE APPLICATION OF DIRECT OBSERVATION IN THE SCHOOL SETTING

From Table 8.1. it is apparent that observation has been used in the assessment of a range of children's problems. In this section, a number of the more frequently cited areas in which it has been applied will be described including the assessment of:
  (i)   disabled children in classroom settings
  (ii)   social skills in children
  (iii) children's learning disabilities
  (iv)   behaviour problems in school

(i) Disabled Children in Classroom Settings

The study of disabled children's classroom behaviour has involved a variety of methodological approaches including social adjustment scales, sociometrics, and teacher judgements. As a number of researchers have pointed out, naturalistic classroom observation is a relatively untried method (Forness, Guthrie, & MacMillan, 1981; Bailey, 1982).

However, the research which has been completed has identified a number of interesting features:
  (a) disabled children exhibit low levels of "spontaneous social behaviour" in classroom situations (Beveridge & Berry, 1977).
  (b) disabled children are characterised by low attending behaviours (Forness & Guthrie, 1977).
  (c) disabled children have difficulty in comprehending and responding to teacher questions (Bailey, 1982).
  (d) teachers of disabled children generally fail to initiate and maintain interactions with the children (Beveridge & Hurrell, 1979).

(e) teachers are very directing and commanding in their interactions with disabled children whilst allowing only a short time for pupil response (Beveridge, Spencer & Mittler, 1978).

From the research conducted so far, it would appear that observation has considerable potential for enhancing our understanding of disabled children's classroom behaviour. Certainly this potential has not been fully exploited to date. More particularly, important questions to address include how different styles of teaching influence disabled children's learning, e.g., how a "directive" style of teaching influences pupil initiation. Certainly observation might be used by teachers of disabled children to better understand their own teaching style or to plan and develop more effective teaching strategies. Bailey (1982) used video-tapes of teacher's interactions with disabled children to these ends in the context of in-service teacher training.

(ii) Social Skills in Children
Considerable attention has been given to the field of social skills assessment in adults (Argyle, 1972) but it is only recently that attention has been given to the study of social skills in children. The assessment of children's social skills is important for a number of reasons:

(a) socially isolated or unpopular children have been found to be deficient in skills such as co-operation, and positive response to peers (Gottman, Gonso, & Schuler, 1976; Odin & Asher, 1977).

(b) inadequate social skills have been associated with poor academic performance (Cartledge & Milburn, 1978).

(c) children deficient in social skills have a high incidence of school maladjustment (Gronlund & Anderson, 1963).

As Gresham (1981, p.125) notes, "... behavioural observations have been frequently used in assessing social skills because of their sensitivity, non-reactivity, and specificity regarding antecedents and consequences of social interaction." As such, systematic observation has an important role to play in the identification of children at risk in terms of social skills.

(iii) Learning Disabilities

There is a growing body of evidence to suggest that teacher observations are very useful in identifying children with learning problems (Haring & Ridgeway, 1967; Bryan & Wheeler, 1972; Forness & Esveldt, 1975; Cantell & Forness, 1982). In classroom observation researchers have found that learning disabled (LD) boys spent about as much time interacting with peers and teachers as non-LD students, but they were twice as likely to be ignored by classmates and teachers and more likely to receive punishing statements from teachers (Bryan, 1974). Bryan, Wheeler, Felcan and Henek (1976) found that LD children made significantly more competitive statements and made and received significantly more rejection statements than non-LD peers. Moreover, LD children made fewer helpful and considerate statements than their non-LD classmates. Overall, the research to date depicts the LD child as less popular and less socially skilled than their non-LD peers.

Observation offers an important means for better understanding the LD child's classroom behaviour. Presently, further work involving direct observation is needed to clarify the means by which the LD child may be identified and to enhance the development of intervention programmes.

(iv) Behaviour Problems in School

As Deno (1980, p.396) notes, "virtually every teacher has at least one student who might be variously described as a "behaviour problem", "inattentive", "hyperactive", "acting out" or "disruptive". Quay (1979) identifies four major constellations of behavioural problems that children may exhibit in school settings. These clusters have been labelled
    (a) conduct disorders,
    (b) personality disorders,
    (c) inadequacy-immaturity, and
    (d) socialised delinquency.
As described by Quay (1979), conduct disorders include disruptiveness, disobedience, fighting, defiance of authority, and other behaviours that are at variance with society's expectations. Personality disorders include shyness, chronic sadness, lack of self confidence, and behaviours that indicate personal distress. Inadequacy-immaturity relates to short attention span, clumsiness and drowsiness to the extent that

the behaviours come to the notice of the teacher. Socialised delinquency includes gang activity, truancy and stealing. An important outcome of the existence of behaviour problems in children concerns the effect on their academic performance. Cantell and Forness (1982) found that 75% of children referred for psychiatric evaluation had severe problems with academic underachievement. Other studies confirm this finding (Rutter, Tizard & Whitmore, 1970; Sturge, 1982). Various indirect methods are available for assessing behaviour problems in children. Questionnaires have been developed for this purpose (Rutter, 1974; Tizard, 1974) as have rating scales (Achenbach, 1979). Systematic observation has also been used to distinguish problem children from other children in the classroom including conduct disordered children (Nelson, 1971) and children with learning disorders (Bryan & Wheeler, 1972; Forness & Esveldt, 1975). Presently though the use of systematic observation in the study of behaviour problems in children in school settings is under-utilized.

OBSERVATION IN THE CLASSROOM

To observe is to "take notice" or "behold with attention". It is 9.30 am. in a year 7 classroom. The children are involved in project work on Greek mythology. A quick glance around the room would suggest to the teacher that the children are working steadily on their projects. Attending more closely though, she might identify groups or clusters of children with four girls cutting and pasting Greek figures from magazines whilst discussing and helping one another. Another group of two boys and three girls are laughing among themselves about something not connected with project work. To one side of the classroom, a boy is staring out of the window onto the playground, lost in thought and with a rather sad expression on his face. Another child is resting at her desk with eyes closed and her head on her folded arms.

For the astute teacher, the children's verbal and non-verbal behaviour offers some insight into what they are thinking and feeling. In its entirety though, the act of observing is a complex task indeed. For this reason the teacher may

focus on a particular aspect of a child's
behaviour, e.g., helping or pro-social behaviour
or a particular child, e.g., the gifted or slow
learner in the class. Of course, narrowing down
the scope of attention influences who, how, when
and what is observed. Generally speaking,
observation in the classroom may be classified in
terms of:
  (a)   child-child behaviour
  (b)   teacher-child behaviour
  (c)   child-inanimate environment (e.g., toys)
        behaviour.
In choosing to make observations in the classroom,
a teacher might look for the following details in
relation to children's behaviour with each other,
the teacher or aspects of the environment.

<u>Setting</u>.   Where does the behaviour occur,
                   e.g., playground, classroom?
                   At what time of the day does
                   the behaviour occur?
<u>Participants</u>.   Who was involved, e.g., another
                   child or group of children or
                   teacher and how many people
                   were involved?
<u>Behaviours</u>.   (a) Facial expressions, e.g.,
                        happy, sad, angry.
                   (b) Bodily movements, e.g.,
                        hitting, touching.
                   (c) Vocalizations, e.g., what
                        was said and how it was
                        said.
                   Consideration might also be
                   given to assessing the
                   frequency with which these
                   behaviours occurred or the
                   sequence in which they were
                   observed.
<u>Participant's Response</u>.
                   What did the other children or
                   teacher(s) do in relation to
                   the child's behaviour? e.g.,
                   move away, engage in play or
                   talk.
<u>Conclusion</u>.   How did the interaction or
                   episode end? e.g., a fight
                   broke out, or the child asked
                   to join the group and so forth.
The broad categories provided here facilitate
the development of means for systematically
observing children and teachers in school
settings. In using systematic observations some

general guidelines to follow include keeping the
system:
- matched to the concern of the teacher
- reliable, so that repeated observations can be made
- simple in order to best record the behaviours
- analysable in terms of determining frequency of the behaviours, their sequencing and so forth.

DESCRIPTION OF SAMPLE OBSERVATION SCHEMES FOR USE IN SCHOOLS

The following three observation schemes illustrate the means by which a teacher might set about making observations in a school setting.

1. Type and Sequencing of Teacher's Questioning Activity

Aim. The purpose of this observation scheme is to provide information about a teacher's questioning style during classroom interaction.

Categories. The coding scheme contains the following categories of questions:
1. Simple recall - memory questions.
2. Convergent - questions having one right acceptable answer.
3. Divergent - questions allowing for the possibility of several right answers.
4. Evaluative - questions involving a judgement or justification.
5. Procedural - questions relating to organization, discipline or structuring of the lesson.

Procedure. The following coding sheet might be used to record the questions asked.

Name of teacher: Date:
Setting: Time observation commenced:
Number of pupils: Time observation ended:

										TOTAL
1.	Simple recall:	X	X	X	X	X	X	X	X	8
2.	Convergent:	X	X							2
3.	Divergent:									
4.	Evaluative:	X	X	X	X	X				5
5.	Procedural:	X								1

Method. Place a mark (**x**) every time a particular question is asked by a teacher against the appropriate category. This method of coding is known as event sampling.

Analysis of the Data. The marked categories can be totalled to obtain the frequency with which the teacher asks various types of questions.

2. **Student Participation Patterns**

Aim. The aim of this observation scheme is to identify the frequency of different types of student participation in class discussion.

Categories. The coding scheme contains the following categories of student behaviour.
1. Raises hand but is not called upon by the teacher
2. Raises hand and is called upon by the teacher
3. Is called upon without raising hand – does not know the answer
4. Is called upon without raising hand – knows the answer
5. Answers without being called upon or raising hand
6. Other.

Procedure. Draw in the seating arrangement in the classroom and identify the teacher (T) and female (F) and male (M) students in the group. Using the appropriate symbol for the categories mark the nature of each student's

participation during a lesson. Leave as blank no
response. An example of a coding sheet used in
this observation is provided below.

Name of teacher: Date:
Setting: Time observation commenced:
Number of pupils: Time observation ended:

$F^{(2,2,)}$	$M^{(6)}$	$F^{(1,1,1)}$	
$M^{(2)}$	M	$F^{(2,2)}$	T
F	M	$F^{(2)}$	
F	$M^{(4,4,4)}$	$M^{(2)}$	
F	$M^{(11,4,1)}$	M	

Analysis of Data. Frequency scores can be
obtained for:
(a) each category of student participation
(b) a comparison of female and male
    participation rates

3. Handicapped Pre-School Children's Behaviour
   Field (1980) has used the following behavioural
   coding scheme (Table 8.2) in her study of
   handicapped pre-school children.

   Table 8.2. Field's (1980) Coding Scheme for Recording Handicapped
   Pre-School Children's Behaviour

   Behaviours directed towards peer, teacher or toy
   Looking   — continuous visual regard
   Smiling   — mouth upturned while looking
   Vocalising   — vocal sounds while looking or in response to
                    vocalisation by other
   Proximity   — within 3' of person
   Touching   — physical contact, including patting, hugging, rubbing
   Offering Toy—   holding out toy in direction of other person
   Sharing Toy —   mutual contact with an object
   Taking Toy —   physically tugging at or removing toy
   Hitting   — forceful physical contact by hand, foot or object
   Crying   — loud continuous wailing

   Non directed or self directed behaviours
   Looking   — at mirror or body parts
   Smiling   — non directed smiling
   Vocalising   — non directed sounds

Table 8.2. (Cont'd.)

Moving	– non directed movement including body rocking, twirling or aimless wandering
Touching	– stereotyped self stimulation such as hand flapping, mouth rubbing, body tapping

Procedure. As described by Field the behaviours recorded were specifically chosen to represent the repertoire of the handicapped child. A one-zero time sampling procedure was used whereby the child was observed for 10 seconds and then 5 seconds were used to record the behaviours observed.

Analysis of Data. In analysing her data, Field used the observations to assess handicapped children's behaviour towards peers, teachers and toys.

Summary
Observation has an important role to play in the assessment process in the school setting. To date though, the potential for using behavioural observation in educational settings has not been fully realised. Currently, the methods for coding and analysing data are still in the process of development. However, in the preceding section a number of guidelines have been provided to assist teachers or researchers in educational settings to develop coding schemes for the assessment of child behaviour.

OBSERVATION IN THE CLINICAL ASSESSMENT OF CHILDREN
The observation of children has long been a routine clinical procedure used in both the diagnostic and therapeutic aspects of child psychology. Recently though, with the development of a range of observational procedures, e.g., baby biographies or event records (see Chapter 4) and the technology for recording behaviour, e.g., video-recorders (see Chapter 6), more attention has been given to the application of direct observation in the clinical assessment of children. Psychologists and social workers in particular, who are concerned with the assessment of children, are showing an increasing awareness of the advantages of direct observation over more

traditional procedures such as interviewing, personality inventories or psychometric testing. In Table 8.3. a selection of studies using direct observation in the clinical assessment of children is presented.

Table 8.3. Selected Studies of Direct Observation in the Clinical Assessment of Children.

Study	Description of Children	Sampling Method	Behaviour	Setting
Forehand, R. et al. (1973)	compliant and noncompliant	event sampling	compliance and noncompliance	clinic playroom
Jason, L. (1976)	normal	one-zero time sampling	reinforcing behaviour	home
Freeman, B. et al. (1978)	autistic	continuous time sampling	verbal and non-verbal behaviour	clinic playroom
Glennon, B. and Weisz, J. (1978)	normal	event sampling	verbal and non-verbal behaviour	clinic playroom
Wildman, R. and Simon, S. (1978)	autistic	continuous time sampling	social interaction	home
Kogan, K. (1980)	handicapped	continuous time sampling	verbal and non-verbal behaviour	clinic playroom
Cohen, N. and Minole, K.	hyperactive	event sampling	verbal behaviour	clinic playroom school
Konstantareas, M. and Homatidis, S. (1984)	conduct disordered	focal sampling	physical aggression verbal aggression prosocial behaviour	clinic playroom

From the studies outlined in Table 8.3. it can be seen that observation has been used in the clinical assessment of a range of childhood problems. In the following discussion three broad groups are considered:

autistic children
problems in parent-child interaction
abused children

Autistic Children

In broad terms, autism is considered to be a severe developmental disturbance characterised by problems in communication and by what Kanner (1943) notes as an "inability to relate". Systematic observation of autistic children has typically involved comparative studies of the behaviour of autistic, normal and handicapped children (Bartak, Rutter & Cox, 1975; Richer, 1976).

The general thrust of such observational research is that autistic children's social behaviour lacks in normal organizational features as well as being different from the behaviour of normal and the behaviour of disturbed children. For example, Richer (1976) summarises the research comparing autistic and non-autistic children, noting that autistic children:

1. engage in very few social interactions
2. act to avoid the possibility of others approaching, e.g., by avoiding eye contact
3. frequently move away from others
4. are rarely aggressive
5. engage in defensive flight behaviour when approached by others.

More recently, research attention has turned to the observational study of the manner in which the autistic child organizes his/her own behaviour (Martini, 1980). Such research is throwing new light on the nature of autistic behaviour. Thus, Martini's (1980) research revealed hitherto unknown qualities of communicative behaviour in autistic children, e.g., the ability to sychronise or co-ordinate their own behaviour.

Systematic observation has considerable application in the study of autistic children. More particularly further research is needed along the lines of Martini's (1980) work. Apart from increasing our understanding of autistic children's behaviour it would facilitate the development of intervention programmes.

Assessing Parent-Child Interaction

In the last decade, researchers have come to realise that in certain instances, an examination of parent-child interaction would facilitate the assessment process. This realisation stems from a growing understanding that from the moment of birth the infant affects its social environment. For example, from birth, the infant is capable of effectively initiating behaviour and is inclined to behave in ways designed to promote contact with other humans (Ainsworth et al, 1971). By means of crying, looking and smiling (among other behaviours), the infant can initiate and maintain interaction. From birth, then, the infant and parent enter into a complex social relationship where the behaviour of each influences and is in turn influenced by that of the other. As Parke (1979, p.17) has noted, "the current zeitgeist ... has clearly shifted to a study of the reciprocity of interaction and the ways that individuals mutually regulate each other during interaction".

Direct observation lends itself to the study of parent-child interaction. A brief examination of the literature shows that systematic observation of parent-child interaction has been made in relation to learning disabled, physically handicapped, emotionally disturbed and normal children (see Table 8.3.). Observation of parent-child interaction in either naturalistic or laboratory settings has been used to assess differences in interaction patterns, plan intervention strategies and evaluate the effectiveness of the interventions. For example, Twentyman and Martin (1978) used systematic observation to assess mother-child problem solving behaviour and devise intervention strategies. Kogan (1970), Kogan, Gordon and Wimberger (1972), Kogan and Wimberger (1971) have used systematic observations extensively in their assessment and training of parents. For example, teaching parents how to alter interactions with their children.

Roberts and Forehand (1978) have evaluated the use of different observation procedures (descriptive-narrative, event recording, time sampling and event recording) in assessing maladaptive parent-child interaction. They conclude from their study that sequential event recording is most advantageous in terms of accurately describing interaction, identifying behaviours to provide a focus for possible interventions, and identifying and evaluating the intervention strategies.

Overall, systematic observation is increasingly recognised by clinicians as having an important role to play in the assessment of parent-child

relations. Careful analysis of the interactions
between parent and child offers considerable
potential for identifying maladaptive
interactions, e.g., parents who do not provide
enough verbal or non-verbal feedback or who are
hyper-critical, developing interventive strategies
and evaluating the effectiveness of the
interventions. Potential also exists for using
recorded observations (e.g., video-tapes) in
parent training. Presently, considerably more
research is needed to develop the application of
systematic observation to parent-child interaction
in order to facilitate the clinician's use of the
method.

Abused Children
In historical context, it is recognised that child
abuse is not a unique product of contemporary
society. For example, infanticide, except among,
Jews and Christians, has a long history as an
accepted means for disposing of sickly or unwanted
children. Justice Kirby (1982) has noted that in
Australia it is virtually impossible to determine
the true incidence of child maltreatment because
of lack of statistics at Federal level. However,
the Royal Commission on Human Relationships (1977)
estimated that the incidence of non-accidental
injury in Australia could be as high as 13,500
instances a year or 37 children per day. Of
particular concern is the finding in a South
Australian survey (1974-75) of a mortality rate of
5-10%. Presently, the problem of identifying
child abuse in Australia is hampered by lack of a
common definition of the problem.
    In recent years, direct observation has
emerged as an important diagnostic tool in
assessing child abuse. For example, Disbrow,
Doerr and Caulfield (1977) found that abusive and
non-abusive parental couples differed on the
factors of (i) perceived communication, (ii)
child's readiness to learn, and (iii) parent
facilitating behaviour during interaction.
Burgess and Conger (1977) report less verbal and
physical interaction in abusive compared with
normal families. Dietrich, Starr and Kaplan
(1980) have developed an observation scheme for
the recording of mother-infant interaction that
has been shown to have some potential as a
diagnostic tool for work with abusive families.
    Currently, there exists considerable scope for
the development of observation schemes for use

with abusive parents. Such schemes would facilitate the identification and treatment of abusive families.

Summary

As McGregor and MacDougall (1979, p.8) note, "most literature on assessment accepts the approach whereby a team of professionals from various disciplines interview, test and observe the child". It is emphasised here that systematic observation has a very considerable role to play in the assessment process. To date though, the development of methods and techniques for observation are in the early phases of development. More particularly, there is a need for the development of schemes that are economical in terms of time and cost which can be used by the clinician. There is also the need for normative data that will facilitate understanding of the nature of the data obtained through observation.

DESCRIPTION OF SAMPLE OBSERVATION SYSTEMS FOR USE IN THE CLINIC

The Interpersonal Behaviour Constructs System.

This observation scheme has undergone some development and refinement (Kogan & Wimberger, 1971; Kogan & Gordon, 1975; Kogan, 1980). The coding system is concerned with the nature of mother-infant interaction as a reciprocal relationship, whereby the behaviour of each influences the behaviour of the other. The scheme is also concerned with the identification of individual communication patterns or styles of interaction. As described by Kogan (1980), the system involves a 22 item checklist of behaviours that are assessed for occurrence or non-occurrence in every 40 second interval.

Three main portions of the checklist assess the focus of the participant's attention (primarily on the other person, his own activity, or joint activity); amount and type of vocal activity (absent, one-sided, responsive) and lead taking (authority, assertiveness or expertise). Remaining items check for (i) positive and negative affect, (ii) non acceptance, (iii) control, and (iv) submissiveness.

The Interpersonal Constructs System has been widely used for assessment purposes with handicapped children (Kogan, Tyler & Turner,

1974; Kogan & Wimberger, 1971). The scheme has also been used for parent training purposes (Kogan et al, 1972; Kogan et al, 1975).

The Potter and Slee Assessment Checklist
This checklist offers a guide to social workers and psychologists involved in the assessment of families in clinical settings. Basically, a checklist consists of a set of statements about behaviours that clinicians might expect to encounter. As such, they are best used when the behaviours expected are known in advance and when there is no need to provide an indication of the frequency and/or quality of the behaviours involved. As described in Chapter 6, the checklist offers the clinician a number of advantages:
1.   it provides the means for recording data rapidly
2.   it serves to remind the observer of the behaviours to look for
3.   it is economical in terms of time and cost.
The Potter and Slee Assessment Checklist (P-SAC) has been developed and used with children and families at the Child and Family Centre of the Adelaide Children's Hospital. This centre provides intensive day treatment for emotionally and behaviourally disturbed children (Cross, Sweeney and Eiserle, 1986). Referrals come from school psychologists, social workers, teachers and psychiatrists in the community.
It is important to emphasise that the P-SAC is an aid for collecting and organizing observational data on families during the initial interview. The information may be filled in during the course of the interview or when writing the case-notes.
In Table 8.4. an outline of the checklist is provided.

Assessing Children

Table 8.4. The Potter and Slee (1986) Assessment Checklist (P-SAC)

Client's Name: Today's Date:

Date of Birth:

Address:

Name of Those Present at Interview:

- -

1.   In this stage of the interview:

    GREETING   . Introduce yourself
    ENGAGEMENT . Describe the purpose of the interview
    AND   . Describe the structure of the interview
    RAPPORT   . Obtain demographic details
              . Put the client(s) at ease
              . Arrange for child to be present or absent for next stage of interview
    NB: * Who sits where and with whom
        * Who speaks first and their manner

2.   In this stage of the interview:

    INFORMATION . Take a history of the child's problem at home and at school
    GATHERING   . Note the onset, frequency, intensity and duration of the problems
    AND   . Note how the problems are managed and by whom and how successfully
    ASSESSMENT . Examine the child's relationships with family members and peers
    PROCESS   . obtain a child profile from family (see text)
              . Have the parent(s)/children specify the changes sought
              . Obtain a history of the family (genogram).
    NB: * Allow both parents to present their views and see child alone
        * Note areas of conflict between parents/parents and siblings
        * Note how each parent views the child's problem
        * Observe the parents willingness to discipline/control the child
        * Observe the child's reactions to parents and therapist

3. SUMMARY   In this stage of the interview:
    OF
    INTERVIEW   . Review the interview
    AND   . Outline your aims for therapy
    NEXT   . Set homework (if any)
    APPOINTMENT . Set date for next interview.

    NB: * Parents' reaction to the interview
        * Child's reaction to attending therapy.

As set out in Table 8.4. the assessment process is conceived of in three phases during the initial interview.

Phase 1. Greeting, Engagement and Rapport. As part of this initial phase, observation is an integral part of the therapist's armatarium. From the moment of the first contact with the family the experienced therapist is utilising his or her powers of observation. Thus, when greeting the family in the waiting room opportunities present themselves for noting information that may provide insight into family dynamics. For example, who has presented for the interview, how are they dressed, who speaks for whom, and who sits with whom. An important function of the first phase of the interview is for the therapist to establish some rapport with the family and help them understand the purpose of the interview.

Phase 2. Information Gathering and Assessment Process. As the interview proper gets under way key features to note include who assumes responsibility for the family, which parent deals with the presenting problem and any areas of disagreement between the parents about how to deal with the child's problem. If the child is present observations of his/her behaviour during the interview might enable an assessment of whether the child is a leader or follower, fearful or sensitive, dominant or submissive, obedient or disobedient and irritable or placid in dealing with the parents (i.e. a child profile). Other points to observe during the interview include whether family members criticise or argue, are prepared to negotiate or compromise and express their feelings. Note might also be made of unspoken family rules (e.g., no-one cries in this family) and whether coalitions or alliances exist (e.g., mother and son vs dad).

Phase 3. Summary of the Interview and the Next Appointment. In drawing the interview to a close observation might be made of the child's attitude toward the therapist (e.g., disrespectful, obedient or aggressive). The family might be set some homework in the form of information gathering for the next interview.

AN OVERVIEW OF THE OBSERVATION PROCESS
As described in this chapter, direct observation
has an important contribution to make in assessing
children across a range of settings. In preparing
to ·make the observations, the following steps
previously described in this book as represented
in Figure 8.1 might serve as a guide.

Figure 8.1. Steps in the Observation Process

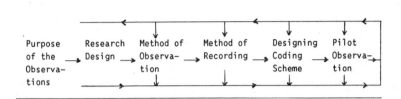

Purpose of the Observations	Research Design	Method of Observation	Method of Recording	Designing Coding Scheme	Pilot Observation

Purpose of the Observations. The teacher/clinician
should give some careful thought as to why the
observations are being made and whether there may
be some more expedient method of gathering the
required information, e.g., questionnaire.

Research Design. In deciding to use direct
observation the question of research design arises.
In Chapter 3 major issues relating to research
design were discussed and the reader is referred
to this chapter.

Methods of Observing. A comprehensive discussion
of the various methods for observing behaviour,
e.g., baby biographies, event sampling, time
sampling and so forth was presented in Chapter 4.

Methods of Recording the Observations. As noted
in Chapter 5, recent technological developments
have increased the options for recording behaviour
(written records, audio-tape, video-tape, and
computer integrated event recorders). Careful
consideration is needed of the most appropriate
method using the guidelines outlined in Chapter 5.

Designing or Adapting an Existing Observation
Scheme. Apart from developing one's own observation scheme, a practical alternative may be to
adapt an existing scheme to one's own requirements.

Conducting Pilot Observations. This important
stage in the observation process provides

opportunity to test the scheme and make the required adjustments. It also provides opportunity to collect reliability data for the scheme. The final product is the observation scheme which can then be used in the observation study.

A CRITIQUE OF DIRECT OBSERVATION

In choosing to use direct observation, the teacher or clinician needs to be aware of the criticisms levelled at the method. The criticisms listed here are by no means exhaustive, but instead represent some of the more major concerns that have been voiced over time.

In the direct observation of behaviour, the focus is upon overt, observable behaviour. There is little room to record the intentions lying behind the behaviour observed. Where such efforts are made the observer usually has to impute intention.

In direct observation, the focus is upon discrete units of behaviour. Coding schemes are typically concerned with "bits of behaviour" rather than with global concepts. As such, meaningful behaviour which might otherwise have contributed to understanding the behaviour observed may be overlooked.

There is a tendency in systematic observation to overlook the context in which the behaviour occurs. Often the observations involve 5-10 minute time periods rather than being collected over hours, days or months. Information about the physical environment in which the behaviour occurs may be overlooked entirely. As such, when the observations are of short duration or separated from their context, interpretation of the meaning of the behaviour is problematic.

The aim of coding schemes using prespecified categories is to produce numerical and normative data. Such data is expected to be suitable for statistical analysis and designed to tell the reader about the "typical" or "average" child or adult behaviour. As such, important information about individual differences may be lost.

In describing these shortcomings of the method it is important to recognise that advocates of the approach would consider them to represent strengths.

CHAPTER SUMMARY
While direct observation may be one of the oldest
forms of scientific enquiry, the popularity of its
use in the clinical fields of the social sciences
has fluctuated widely. Problems militating
against its use include practical considerations
such as the time and cost involved and its labour
intensive nature. Methodologically, problems are
encountered in relation to establishing
reliability, the reactivity of those under
observation, the establishment of normative data
and the generalizability of behaviour across
settings. Acknowledged advantages of direct
observation include the immediacy and firsthand
nature of the data. The method also allows the
clinician to identify sequences of behaviour and
to plan interventions based on observed
interaction between individuals. Recent
technological breakthroughs in terms of recording
procedures, data storage and retrieval and
computer analysis have encouraged renewed interest
in the use of direct observation in the assessment
of children. The way is now open to consolidate
the use of direct observation as an integral part
of the clinician's armatarium in the assessment
process.

Chapter Nine

TOWARD A SCIENCE OF CHILD OBSERVATION

In proportion as he simplifies his life, the
laws of the universe will appear less complex
and solitude will not be solitude, nor poverty
poverty, nor weakness weakness. If you have
built castles in the air, your work need not
be lost; that is where they should be. Now
put the foundations under them (Thoreau, 1960,
p.215).

INTRODUCTION
The science of child observation stands at the
threshold of new and exciting developments.
Within the social sciences there is a growing
interest in the field from various disciplines
engaged in the study of child development. For
example, teachers are becoming more aware of the
important role observation plays in understanding
classroom dynamics, teaching behaviour and in
assessing children's emotional, social and
cognitive development. In other disciplines
social workers and psychologists utilise direct
observation in the assessment and counselling of
children and their families.

Evidence has been presented in this book that
considerable developments have occurred in the
methods used to record and collect observational
data. From the point where interested observers
recorded hand written diary type accounts of
children's behaviour, methods have developed to
include audio and video taping of observations.
Technological breakthroughs have also occurred in
relation to computer assisted collation and
analysis of data.

However, a major thrust of the argument
presented in the present text is that, while
methods and procedures have been developed and
refined the underpinning philosophy of science has

not altered all that much. The philosophical foundation for much of contemporary child observation methods still draws heavily upon a positivist/empiricist outlook. However, the limitations of this paradigm are increasingly being emphasised in contemporary philosophy of science writings. At this point it is important to note that the intention in this book is not to throw the empiricist baby out with the new paradigm bath water. Rather, as will become evident in this chapter, the emphasis is on obtaining the best possible account and understanding of children's behaviour. From this writer's perspective, such a task entails obtaining the greatest possible understanding of the 'inner' person's view of the world and their behaviour as opposed to the 'outer' (observer's) interpretation of the person's world and their behaviour. As Bullivant (1978, p.242) so concisely expresses the sentiment of this book, "... it would be a mistake to abandon everything that smacks of positivism. Many aspects of social life lend themselves to quantitative measures ...".

In this concluding chapter, the intention is to draw together a number of rather disparate ideas concerning the nature of child observation expressed in the preceding chapters. A framework is outlined for conceptualising the observation process. The purpose of this framework is to provide students and teachers of child observation with the means for evaluating and conducting observational studies.

A FRAMEWORK FOR OBSERVATIONAL RESEARCH
In Figure 9.1. the major dimensions of observational research identified in this book are presented.

Toward a Science of Child Observation

Figure 9.1. A Framework for Observational Research

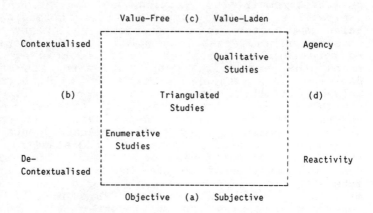

The dimensions in Figure 9.1. relate to:
1. characteristics of the observation process (dimensions a, b, c) and
2. characteristics of the person (dimension d).

The dimensions in Figure 9.1. are by no means intended to represent all facets of the observation process but, in terms of the current philosophy of science debate they are significant. In this text the dimensions have been previously touched upon in Chapters 1 and 5 although the following discussion owes much to pertinent articles written by Ray Rist (1977) and Judith Goetz and Margret LeCompte (1981).

The Objective-Subjective Dimension

At the heart of any debate on methodology, is the issue of objectivity. Empiricism emphasises the 'brute' nature of data. As such, data are considered to be facts about the world that can be identified and recorded in an objective, value-free, presuppositionless manner by neutral observers. While objectivity is the sine qua non of quantitative research methods, qualitative approaches emphasise the more subjective aspects of knowledge. From a subjective perspective, consideration rests with obtaining an 'inside view' of the person and on understanding a person's attitudes, beliefs, values and world view.

Toward a Science of Child Observation

The Contextualised-Decontextualised Dimension
Considerable research ·in the social sciences,
especially that derived from an empirical/
positivist outlook, tends to record and interpret
behaviour apart from context. Alternatively, the
more interpretive methods for understanding
behaviour (e.g., hermeneutics) emphasise that the
meaning of behaviour cannot be understood apart
from its context.

Value-Free/Value-Laden Dimension
The traditional is (facts) - ought (values) distinction in moral philosophy identifies another
important dimension in observational studies.
From a positivist/empiricist perspective,
mainstream science emphasises the value-free
nature of scientific enquiry. However, more
interpretive methodologies acknowledge that facts
are value-laden and that values are
under-determined by facts.

The Agency dimension
From an empirical perspective the individual is
viewed as essentially a passive, reactive organism
in relation to environmental stimuli. The notion
of agency refers to an individual's power to
control and initiate change, and to make choices
perhaps based on values. The view of the person
as an agent reflects a more interpretive outlook
in the social sciences.
     Each of the four observational research
dimensions presented. here are represented as
continua. In reviewing various studies then, it
is possible for the interested reader to locate
characteristics of the studies along the various
dimensions. Studies may overlap along the
dimensions or combine different combinations of
the dimensions. In the following section three
illustrative approaches to research are described
which incorporate the four dimensions outlined
here, namely, (i) enumerative, (ii) triangulated
and (iii) qualitative studies.

ENUMERATIVE STUDIES
Enumerative studies (Goetz & LeCompte, 1981)
reflect mainstream empirical methodology.
Emphasis is given to frequency counts, objective
description of behaviour and precise definition.
Typically, enumerative studies serve to test
rather than generate hypotheses. Consideration is

given to the idea that knowledge is cumulative, and verification of generalisations about the natural world are given priority. From an empirical perspective, enumerative studies represent the method for the conduct of scientific enquiry.

Within a more qualitative tradition an enumerative approach may serve the purpose of supplementing descriptive data or stand by itself as data gathering procedure (Goetz and LeCompte, 1981). An example of the latter purpose is provided in a study by LeCompte (1978) where an enumerative approach was used to test hypotheses about teacher behaviour that had been generated using ethnographic procedures. In her study LeCompte used a category system of data collection that recorded as much behaviour as possible with minimal observer inference. Thus, 41 specific types of teacher verbal and non-verbal behaviour provided the basis for the coding scheme.

In employing the dimensions outlined in Figure 9.1. it can be seen that enumerative studies would emphasise the objective, value-free nature of data where the meaning of behaviour would be interpreted independent of the context in which it occurred. The issue of the person's agency would not figure prominently.

TRIANGULATED STUDIES
The triangulated data gathering strategy, also referred to as 'supplemented participatory observation' (Bullivant, 1978) is a procedure for combining various research methods in the investigation of a problem. Thus, quantitative and qualitative methods are conceived of as complementary and hence combined where possible. For example, a researcher might utilise quantitative data gathered from a questionnaire and more qualitative data gleaned from unstructured interviews or participant observation. Whyte (1955) expresses a strong preference for triangulation in observational studies noting a common complaint of researchers, namely the polarisation of quantitative and qualitative research strategies has served to preclude opportunities for researchers to benefit from the advantages each method has to offer. Denzin (1978, p.28) has also used the term "triangulation", noting:

I concluded that no single method will ever permit an investigator to develop causal propositions free of rival interpretations. Similarly, I conclude that no single method will ever meet the requirements of interaction theory. While participant observation permits the careful recording of situations and selves, it does not offer direct data on the wider spheres of influence acting on those observed. Because each method reveals different aspects of empirical reality, multiple methods of observation must be employed. This is termed triangulation.

Denzin has noted that there are four basic types of triangulation including:

1. data triangulation, with information collected on (i) time, (ii) space and (iii) people involved.
2. investigator triangulation which emphasises the use of multiple rather than single observers.
3. theory triangulation which calls for the use of multiple rather than single perspectives in an attempt to better understand the nature of the observed phenomenon.
4. methodological triangulation which calls for the use of different methods in the study of any phenomenon.

As is apparent from Denzin's work, triangulated studies focus researchers' attention upon the need to gather data from different sources, using multiple methods whilst viewing reality as complex and multi-faceted. The approach emphasises that quite apart from the accepted empirical ways of understanding the world around us it is imperative to use other data sources typically overlooked in the scientific endeavour. In their seminal paper on the implications of the new philosophy of science for psychology, Manicas and Secord (1983, p.410) note "... whether palatable or not, scientific knowledge is much closer to knowledge that is more familiarly accessible through common sense, literature and other modes of experience".

In terms of Figure 9.1., triangulation refers to the need to combine methods. As Whyte (1955, p.216) has noted, the strategy "... calls for a weaving back and forth among methods through the various stages of research". To this end, the various dimensions in Figure 9.1. might be used in various combinations through different phases of a particular research project.

QUALITATIVE STUDIES

At one extreme, representatives of this strategy, such as the philosopher Feyerbend (1975), conceive of science as an ideology for which only historical or cultural explanations can be given. Essentially though, the qualitative type of research utilises methods and techniques of observing, recording, analysing and interpreting facets, patterns, characteristics and meanings of behaviour as part of the total context under study. The focus is upon explicating the qualitative features of the phenomenon under study, e.g., the symbols, rituals and experiences that contribute to the essence of the phenomenon. A major objective of this type of research is to document and understand as fully as possible the situation from the other's frame of reference. In terms of the dimensions outlined in Figure 9.1. emphasis is given to understanding the values, world views and meaning systems guiding a person's behaviour. The individual would be viewed very much as an agent and the interpretation of behaviour could not be viewed apart from the context in which it occurred. In describing the major characteristics of qualitative research Leininger (1985, p.6) notes:

> Qualitative research is often the initial way to discover phenomenon and to document unknown features of some aspect of people, events or the life setting of people under study. It is the major research method - to discover essences, feelings, attributes, values, meanings, characteristics, and teleological or philosophical aspects of certain individuals or group lifeways ... Grasping the totality of how events, situations and experiences fit together and form the people's viewpoint and world view is a major feature of qualitative research.

CHAPTER SUMMARY

Utilising the four major dimensions of

observational research outlined in Figure 9.1, a model has been constructed to facilitate understanding of the observational research endeavour. As outlined in Chapter 8, determining the purpose for which the observations are being made is the first step which then ultimately affects the choice of the type of study conducted. It is strongly argued here that the subsequent steps involving the research design and method of observation are profoundly theoretical. That is, the choices made reflect an identifiable, if implicit body of theory. It should be incumbent upon the researcher to explicate the theoretical underpinnings of the study. To this end the nature of the research strategy chosen, e.g., enumerative or triangulated would be more clearly identified. In outlining the framework for the research strategy reference could then be made to major dimensions (e.g., objective-subjective, agency) influencing the research outcome.

EPILOGUE

> To see a World in a grain of sand
> And a Heaven in a wild flower,
> Hold Infinity in the palm of your Hand
> And Eternity in an hour
>   (W. Blake).

As reflected in the first stanza of William Blake's "Auguries of Innocence" quoted above, the art of observation or the ability to see deeply into the nature of things, would indeed open up new worlds for us. Furthermore, it is an art encouraged not only in the sciences. For example, the dramatist/writer Stanslavski (1948, p.86) noted that:

> An actor should be observant not only on the stage but also in real life. He should concentrate with all his being on whatever attracts his attention. He should look at an object, not as any absent-minded passerby, but with penetration. Otherwise his whole creative method will prove lopsided and bear no relationship to life.

Within the physical and social sciences direct

observation is a cornerstone of the methods by which we seek to understand the world around us. To paraphrase Stanslavski, the task confronting those involved in child observation research, is to develop the means for observing in as penetrative a way as possible in order that the child's behaviour should bear the strongest possible relationship to life.

Presently, the developing science of child observation stands on the threshold of new and exciting times. Aspects of the new heuristic will accommodate a broader vision of science and will move to elucidate a clearer philosophical framework for observational research. In a holistic sense there will emerge a richer and more humane approach to child study.

> I love a broad margin to my life. Sometimes, in a summer morning, having taken my accustomed bath, I sat in my sunny doorway from sunrise till noon, rapt in a revery, amidst the pines and hickories and sumachs, in undisturbed solitude and stillness, while the birds sang around or flitted noiseless through the house, until by the sun falling in at my west window, or the noise of some traveller's wagon on the distant highway, I was reminded of the lapse of time. I grew in these seasons like corn in the night, and they were far better than any work of the hands would have been. They were not times subtracted from my life, but so much over and above my usual allowance.
>
> (Thoreau, 1960, p.79).

REFERENCES

Abercrombie, M.L.J. (1969), The Anatomy of Judgement, Harmondsworth : Penguin.

Achenbach, T.M. (1979), The child behaviour profile: An empirically based system for assessing children's behavioural problems and competencies, International Journal of Mental Health, I, 24-42.

Ainsworth, M.D., Bell, S.M. and Stayton, D.J. (1971), Individual differences in strange-situation behaviour of one-year-olds IN H.R. Schaffer (Ed.), The origins of human social relations, New York : Academic Press.

Altman, J. (1974), Observational study of behaviour : Sampling Methods, Behavior, 49, 227-65.

Anderson, B.J. and Vietze, P.M. (1977), Early Dialogues : The structure of reciprocal infant-mother vocalisation IN S. Cohen and T.J. Comiskey (Eds), Child Development. Contemporary Perspectives, Itasca, Illinois: Peacock Publishers.

Argyle, M. (1972), The Psychology of Interpersonal Behaviour, London : Pelican.

Aries, P. (1962), Centuries of Childhood, New York : Vintage Books.

Australian Royal Commission on Human Relationships (1977), Final Report, Canberra : Australian Government Publishing Service.

Axline, V. (1964), Dibs: In Search of Self, London : Pelican.

Bailey, L. (1982), A Study of Children With Multiple Disabilities, Unpublished Report. South Australian Institute of Technology.

Bailey, L. and Slee, P.T. (1984), A comparison of play interactions between non-disabled and disabled children and their mothers : A question of style, Australian and New Zealand Journal of Developmental Disabilities, 10, 5-10.

135

References

Barker, R.G. (1963), The Stream of Behaviour, New York : Appleton-Century-Crofts.

Barker, R.G. (1968), Ecological Psychology: Concepts and Methods for Studying the Environment of Human Behaviour, Stanford University Press.

Barker, R.G. and Wright, H.R. (1955), Midwest and its Children : The Psychological Ecology of an American Town, New York : Row and Peterson.

Bartak, L., Rutter, M. and Cox, A. (1975), A comparative study of infantile autism and specific developmental receptive language disorder, British Journal of Psychiatry, 126, 127-45.

Battye, P. and Slee, P.T. (1985), The demise of the person in social work, Australian Social Work, 38, 23-31.

Beveridge, M.C. and Berry, P. (1977), Observing interactions in severely mentally handicapped children, Research in Education, 19, 39-48.

Beveridge, M., and Hurrell, P. (1979), Teacher's responses to severely mentally handicapped children's initiations in the classroom, Journal of Child Psychology and Psychiatry, 21, 175-81.

Beveridge, M., Spencer, J. and Mittler, P. (1978), Language and social behaviour in severely educationally subnormal children, British Journal of Social and Clinical Psychology, 17, 75-83.

Blair, L. (1976), Rhythms of Vision, London: Paladin.

Blake, W. (1971), Songs of Innocence, Great Britain : Dover Publications, Inc.

Blake, W. (1981), Auguries of innocence, IN A.P. Wavell, Other Men's Flowers, Harmondsworth : Penguin.

Brandt, R.M. (1972), Studying Behaviour in Natural Setting, New York : Holt, Rinehart and Winston.

Brazelton, T.B., Koslowski, B. and Main, M. (1974), The origins of reciprocity : The early mother-infant interaction IN M. Lewis and L.A. Rosenblum (Eds), The Effect of the Infant on its Caregiver, New York : John Wiley and Sons.

Brazelton, T.B., Tronick, E., Adamson, L., Als, H. and Wise, S. (1975), Early mother-infant reciprocity IN Parent-Infant Interaction, CIBA Foundation Symposium.

Bronfenbrenner, U. (1977), Toward an experimental ecology of human development, American Psychologist, 32, 513-31.

References

Brown, J.E. and Slee, P.T. (1987), Paradoxical Interventions : The ethics of intervention, Professional Psychology : Research and Practice. (In press).

Bryan, T.S. (1974), An observational analysis of classroom behaviours of children with learning disabilities, Journal of Learning Disabilities, 7, 35-43.

Bryan, T.S. and Wheeler, R. (1972), Perception of learning disabled children : The eye of the observer, Journal of Learning Disabilities, 5, 484-8.

Bryan, T., Wheeler, R., Felcan, J. and Henek, T. (1976), Come on, Dummy : An observational study of children's communications, Journal of Learning Disabilities, 9, 53-61.

Bullivant, B.M. (1978), Towards a neo-ethnographic method for small-group research, Australian and New Zealand Journal of Sociology, 14, 239-49.

Bullowa, M. (1975), When infant and adult communicate how do they sychronise their behaviours, IN A. Kendon, R.M. Harris and M.R. Key (Eds), Organisation of Behaviour in Face-to-Face Interaction, New York : Mouton Publishers.

Burgess, R.L. and Conger, R.D. (1977), Family Interaction in Abusive, Neglectful and Normal Families. Paper presented at the meeting of the Society for Research in Child Development, New Orleans : March.

Burnett, J.H. (1967), Description and analysis in the micro-ethnography of urban classrooms, IN J. Roberts and S. Akinsanya (Eds), Educational Patterns and Cultural Configurations, New York : David McKay Company.

Cairns, R.B. and Green, J.A. (1979), How to assess personality and social patterns: Observations or ratings? IN R.B. Cairns (Ed.), The Analysis of Social Interactions: Methods, Issues and Illustrations, New York: Lawrence Erlbaum Associates.

Cantell, D. and Forness, S.R. (1982), Learning disorders, Journal of American Academy of Child Psychiatry, 21, 417-19.

Capra, F. (1982), The Turning Point. Science, Society and the Rising Culture, ʽNew York: Fontana.

Capra, F. (1982), The Tao of Physics, Great Britain : Oxford Uni. Press.

References

Carraher, T., Carraher, D. and Schliemann, A.
(1985), Mathematics in street and schools,
The British Journal of Developmental Psychol-
ogy, 3, 21-31.
Cartledge, G. and Milburn, J.F. (1978), The case
for teaching social skills in the classroom.
A review, Review of Educational Research, 48,
133-56.
Castellan, N.J. (1979), The analysis of behaviour
sequences, IN R.B. Cairns (Ed.), The Analysis
of Social Interactions : Methods, Issues and
Illustrations, New York : Lawrence Erlbaum
Associates.
Caudill, W. (1958), The Psychiatric Hospital as a
Small Society, Cambridge, Mass. : Harvard
University Press.
Clarke-Stewart, K.A. and Hevey, C.M. (1981),
Longitudinal relations in repeated observations
of mother-child interaction from 1 to 2-1/2
years, Developmental Psychology, 17, 127-45.
Collier, J. (1973), Alaskan Eskimo Education : A
Film Analysis of Cultural Confrontation in the
Schools, New York : Holt, Rinehart and
Winston.
Compayre, G. (1896), The intellectual and moral
development of the child, Mary Wilson, trans.
New York : Appleton.
Cross, D.G., Sweeney, J. and Eiserle, E. (1985-6),
Conduct-disordered children 1. A review,
Records of the Adelaide Children's Hospital,
3, 244-9.
Darwin, C. (1965), The Expression of the Emotions
in Man and Animals, The University of Chicago
Press.
Davies, P. (1982), Other worlds. Space, Super-
space and the Quantum Universe, London:
Abacus.
Davies, W.H. (1981), Leisure, IN A.P. Wavell,
Other Men's Flowers, London : Penguin.
Dawe, H.C. (1934), An analysis of two hundred
quarrels of preschool children, Child
Development, 5, 139-157.
Delamont, S. (1984), Readings on Interaction in
the Classroom, London : Methuen.
DeMaria, W. (1981), Empiricism : An impoverished
philosophy for social science research,
Australian Social Work, 34, 3-8.
Deno, S. (1980), Direct observation approach to
measuring classroom behaviour, Exceptional
Children, 2, 396-9.

References

Denzin, N.K. (1978), The Research Act : A
Theoretical Introduction to Sociological
Methods, New York : McGraw-Hill.

Dickens, C. (1968), Hard Times, New York:
Holt, Rinehart and Winston.

Dietrich, K., Starr, R. and Kaplan, M. (1980),
Maternal stimulation and care of abused
infants IN F.M. Field, S. Goldberg,
D. Stern and A.M. Sostek, High-Risk Infants
and Children. Adult and Peer Interactions,
New York : Academic Press.

Disbrow, M.A., Doerr, H.O. and Caufield, C.
(1977), Measures to Predict Abuse. Final
Report on Maternal and Child Health Grant
MC-R530351. Seattle, Washington : University of Washington.

Eisler, R.M., Hersen, M. and Agras, W.S. (1973),
Videotape : A method for the controlled
observation of non-verbal interpersonal
behaviour, Behaviour Therapy, 4, 420-5.

Erikson, K. (1967), A comment on disguised
observation in sociology, Social Problems,
14, 366-73.

Evans, C.S. (1979), Preserving the Person : A
Look at the Human Sciences, I.V.P., Illinois,
1979.

Farson, R. (1974), MS. Magazine, March 11,
66-7.

Festinger, L. and Katz, D. (1953), Research
Methods in the Behavioural Sciences, New
York : Holt, Rinehart and Winston.

Feyerbend, P. (1975), Against Method, London:
NLB.

Field, T.M., Goldberg, S., Stern, D. and Sostek,
A.M. (1980), High Risk Infants and Children,
New York : Academic Press.

Field, T. (1980), Self, teacher, toy and
peer-directed behaviours of handicapped
preschool children, IN T.M. Field,
S. Goldberg, D. Stern and A.M. Sostek (Eds),
High-Risk Infants and Children. Adult and
Peer Interactions, New York : Academic Press.

Flanders, N. (1970), Analysing Teacher Behaviour,
Reading, Mass. : Addison-Wesley.

Fogel, A. (1977), Temporal organisation in
mother-infant face-to-face interaction, IN
H.R. Schaffer (Ed.), Studies in Mother-Infant
Interaction, New York : Academic Press.

Fordham, F. (1971), An Introduction to Jung's
Psychology, London : Pelican.

References

Forehand, R., King, E., Peed, S. and Yoder, P.
(1973), Mother-child interactions : Comparison
of a non compliant clinic group and a
non-clinic group, Behaviour Research and
Therapy, 13, 79-84.

Forness, S.R. and Guthrie, D. (1977), Stability
of short-term classroom observations,
Psychology in the Schools, 14, 116-20.

Forness, S.R. and Esveldt, K. (1975), Classroom
observation of children with learning and
behaviour problems, Journal of Learning
Disabilities, 8, 49-52.

Forness, S.R., Guthrie, D. and MacMillan, D.
(1981), Classroom behaviour of mentally
retarded children across different classroom
settings, The Journal of Special Education,
15, 497-509.

Fraser, B.G. (1976), The child and his parents:
A delicate balance of rights, IN R. Helfer
and C.H. Kempe (Eds), Child Abuse and Neglect,
Cambridge, Mass. : Ballinger Pub. Co.

Freeman, B., Ritvo, E., Guthrie, D., Schroth, P.
and Ball, J. (1978), The behaviour observation
scale for autism, Journal of the American
Academy of Child Psychiatry, 17, 576-88.

Gaensbauer, T.J. and Mrazek, D. (1981),
Differences in patterning of affective
expression in infants, Journal of American
Academy of Child Psychology, 20, 673-91.

Gaensbauer, T.J., Mrazek, D. and Emde, R.N.
(1979), Patterning of emotional responses in
a playroom laboratory situation, Infant
Behaviour and Development, 2, 163-78.

Gardner, R.A. (1975), Psychotherapeutic
Approaches to the Resistant Child, New York:
Jason Aronson Inc.

Gauld, A. and Shotter, J. (1977), Human Action and
its Psychological Investigation, London:
Routledge and Kegan Paul.

Glennon, B. and Weisz, J. (1978), An observational
approach to the assessment of anxiety in young
children, Journal of Consulting and Clinical
Psychology, 46, 1246-57.

Goetz, J.P. and LeCompte, M.D. (1981), Ethnographic research and the problem of data
reduction, Anthropology and Education
Quarterly, 12, 51-70.

Gold, R. (1958), Roles in sociological field
observations, Social Forces, 36, 217-23.

References

Goodenough, F. (1931), The expressions of emotions in infancy, Child Development, 2, 96-101.

Gottman, J.M. and Bakeman, R. (1979), The sequential analysis of observational data, IN M.E. Lamb, S.S. Suomi and G.R. Stephenson (Eds), Social Interaction Analysis. Methodological Issues, The University of Wisconsin Press.

Gottman, J., Gonso, J. and Schuler, P. (1976), Teaching social skills to isolated children, Journal of Abnormal Child Psychology, 4, 179-97.

Gresham, F.M. (1981), Assessment of children's social skills, Journal of School Psychology, 19, 120-33.

Gronlund, H. and Anderson, L. (1963), Personality characteristics of socially accepted, socially neglected, and socially rejected junior high school pupils, IN J. Seiderman (Ed.), Educating for Mental Health, New York: Crowell.

Gunnar, M.R. and Donahue, M. (1980), Sex differences in social responsiveness between six months and twelve months, Child Development, 51, 262-5.

Harré, R. and Secord, P.F. (1972), The Explanation of Social Behaviour, Oxford : Basil Blackwell.

Harmid, A. (1952), Outlines of Roman Law, New Delhi Press.

Haring, N. and Ridgeway, R. (1967), Early identification of children with learning disabilities, Exceptional Children, 33, 387-98.

Hartup, W.W. (1979), Levels of analysis in the study of social interaction : An historical perspective, IN M. Lamb, S.J. Suomi and G.R. Stephenson (Eds), Social Interaction Analysis. Methodological Analysis, University of Wisconsin Press, 1979.

Haskell, E.M. (Ed.) (1896), Child Observations: First Series : Imitation and Allied Activities, Boston : Heath.

Heather, N. (1976), Radical Perspectives in Psychology, London : Methuen.

Heidelise, A., Tronick, E. and Brazelton, T.B. (1979), Analysis of face-to-face interaction in infant-adult dyads, IN M. Lamb, S.J. Suomi, and G.R. Stephenson (Eds), Social Interaction Analysis. Methodological Issues, The University of Wisconsin Press.

141

References

Hinde, R.A. (1973), On the design of checksheets, *Primates*, 14, 393-406.

Hobbes, T. (1931), *Leviathan*, Oxford : Basil Blackwell.

Holland, C.J. (1970), An interview guide for behavioural counselling with parents, *Behaviour Therapy*, 1, 70-9.

Horrocks, J.E. (1964), *Assessment of Behaviour*, Charles E. Merrill.

Izard, C.E. (1971), *The Face of Emotion*, New York : Appleton-Century-Crofts.

Jason, L.A. (1976), Recording parent-child interactional patterns, *Perceptual and Motor Skills*, 42, 279-82.

Johnson, S.M. and Bolstadt, O.D. (1973), Methodological issues in naturalistic observation. Some problems and solutions for field research, IN L.A. Hamerlynch, L.C. Handy and E.J. Mash (Eds), *Behavioural Changes and Methodological Concepts and Practice*, Canada : Banff.

Jones, B. (1963), *The psycho-epistemological profile: its scoring validity and reliability*, Ph.D. Thesis, University of Alberta.

Jones, O.H.M. (1980), Prelinguistic communication skills in Down's syndrome and normal infants, IN T.M. Field, S. Goldberg, D. Stern and A.M. Sostek (Eds), *High Risk Infants and Children. Adult and Peer Interactions*, New York : Academic Press.

Kanner, L. (1943), Autistic disturbances of affective contact, *Nervous Child*, 2, 217-50.

Kerlinger, F. (1973), *Foundations of Behavioural Research*, London : Holt, Rinehart and Winston.

Kessen, W. (1965), *The Child*, New York : Wiley.

Kirby, M.D. (1982), Child abuse : What can the law do? *Australian Journal of Early Childhood*, 7, 4-12.

Koan, S. and McGuire, W.S. (1973), The yin and yang of progress in social psychology, *Journal of Personality and Social Psychology*, 26, 446-56.

Kogan, K. (1980), Interaction systems between preschool handicapped or developmentally delayed children and their parents, IN T.M. Field, S. Goldberg, D. Stern and A. Sostek (Eds), *High Risk Infants and Children. Adult and Peer Interactions*. New York : Academic Press.

References

Kogan, K.L. (1970), Specificity and stability of mother-child interaction styles, Child Psychology and Human Development, 2, 160-8.

Kogan, K.L. and Gordon, B.N. (1975), Interpersonal behaviour constructs : A revised approach to defining dyadic interaction styles, Psychological Reports, 36, 835-46.

Kogan, K.L. and Wimberger, H.C. (1971), Behaviour transactions between disturbed children and their mothers, Psychological Reports, 28, 395-404.

Kogan, K.L., Gordon, B.W. and Wimberger, H.C. (1972), Teaching Mothers to alter interactions with their children : Implications for those who work with children and parents, Childhood Education, 49, 107-10.

Kogan, K.L., Tyler, N. and Turner, P. (1974), The process of interpersonal adaption between mothers and their cerebral palsied children, Developmental Medicine and Child Neurology, 16, 518-27.

Kogan, K.L., Wimberger, H.C. and Bobbitt, R.A. (1969), Analysis of mother-child interaction in young mental retardates, Child Development, 40, 799-812.

Konstantareas, M. and Homatidis, S. (1984), Aggressive and prosocial behaviours before and after treatment in conduct-disordered children and in matched controls, Journal of Child Psychology and Psychiatry, 25, 4, 608-20.

Kuhn, T.S. (1970), The Structure of Scientific Revolutions, University of Chicago Press.

Lamb, M., Suomi, S.J. and Stephenson, G. (1979), Social Interaction Analysis. Methodological Issues, The University of Wisconsin Press.

LeCompte, M. (1978), Learning to work : The hidden curriculum of the classroom, Anthropology and Education Quarterly, 9, 22-37.

LeCompte, M. and Goetz, J. (1982), Problems of reliability and validity in ethnographic research, Review of Educational Research, 52, 31-60.

Leininger, M. (1985), Qualitative Research Methods in Nursing, New York : Grune and Stratton.

Lewis, M. and Lee-Painter, S. (1974), An interactional approach to the mother-infant dyad, IN M. Lewis and L.A. Rosenblum (Eds), The Effect of the Infant on its Caregiver, New York : John Wiley and Sons.

References

Liebert, R.M. and Baron, R.A. (1972), Short-term effects of televised aggression on children's aggressive behaviour, IN Television and Social Behaviour, Rockville, Md : U.S. Dept. of Health Education and Welfare.

Lipinski, D. and Nelson, R. (1974), Problems in the use of naturalistic observation as a means of behavioural assessment, Behaviour Therapy, 5, 341-51.

Lobitz, G.K. and Johnson, S.M. (1975), Normal versus deviant children : A multi method comparison, Journal of Abnormal Child Psychology, 3, 353-74.

London, P. (1964), The Modes and Morals of Psychotherapy, New York : Holt, Rinehart and Winston.

Lyon, D. (1982), Valuing in social science : Post empiricism and Christian responses. (Unpub.)

Lytton, H. (1980), Parent-Child Interaction. The Socialisation Process Observed in Twin and Singleton Families, New York : Plenum Press.

Lytton, H. and Zwirner, W. (1975), Compliance and its controlling stimuli observed in a natural setting, Developmental Psychology, 11, 769-79.

MacFarlane, A.C. and Raphael, B. (1984), Ash Wednesday : The effects of a fire, Australian and New Zealand Journal of Psychiatry, 18, 341-51.

Manicas, P. and Secord, P. (1983), Implications for psychology of the new philosophy of science, American Psychologist, 4, 399-413.

Martin, M.F., Gefland, D.M. and Hartman, D.P. (1971), Effects of adult and peer observers on boys' and girls' responses to an aggressive model, Child Development, 42, 1271-5.

Martini, M. (1980), Structures of interaction between two autistic children, IN T.M. Field, S. Goldberg, D. Stern, A.M. Sostek (Eds), High-Risk Infants and Children. Adult and Peer Interactions, New York : Academic Press.

Massie, H.N. (1980), Pathological interactions in infancy, IN T.M. Field, S. Goldberg, D. Stern, A.M. Sostek (Eds), High-Risk Infants and Children, New York : Academic Press.

Mayo, C. and La France, M. (1978), On the acquisition of non verbal communication: A review, Merrill-Palmer Quarterly, 24, 213-28.

Medinnus, G.R. (1976), Child Study and Observation Guide, New York : John Wiley and Sons.

References

Medley, D.M. and Mitzel, H.E. (1963), Measuring class-room behaviour by systematic observation, IN N.L. Gage (Ed.), Handbook of Research on Teaching, Chicago : Rand McNally.

Mehan, H. (1979), Learning Lessons, Harvard : The University Press.

Milton, J. (1951), Paradise Lost, and selected poetry and prose, F. Northrop (Ed.), New York : Holt, Rinehart and Winston.

McGregor, S., MacDougall, C.J. (1979), The Development of Assessment Panels in South Australia. Unpublished Paper.

Nelson, C.M. (1971), Techniques for screening conduct disturbed children, Exceptional Children, 37, 501-7.

Newson, J. (1977), An intersubjective approach to the systematic description of mother-infant interaction, IN H.R. Schaffer (Ed.), Studies in Mother-Infant Interaction, New York : Academic Press.

Novak, M., Olley, J.G., Kearney, D. (1980), Social skills of children with special needs in integrated separate pre-schools, IN T.M. Field, S. Goldberg, D. Stern and A.M. Sostek (Eds), High Risk Infants and Children, New York : Academic Press.

Odin, S. and Asher, S.R. (1977), Coaching children in social skills for friendship making, Child Development, 48, 495-506.

Oppenheim, A.N. (1966), Questionnaire Design and Attitude Measurement, London : Heinemann.

Oxenberry, R. (1976), Children - their status in the community and the approach to child welfare, Australian Child and Family Welfare, 1, 10-13.

Palermo, D.S. (1971), Is a Scientific Revolution Taking Place in Psychology? Science Studies, 1, 135-55.

Park, C.C. (1967), The Seige, Harmondsworth: Pelican Books.

Parke, R.D. (1979), Interactional designs, IN R.B. Cairns (Ed.), The Analysis of Social Interactions : Methods, Issues and Illustrations, New York : Lawrence Erlbaum Associates.

Parke, R.D. (1978), Parent-infant interaction: Progress, paradigms and problems, IN G.P. Sackett (Ed.), Observing Behaviour. Vol. 1. Theory and Applications in Mental Retardation, Baltimore, Md : University Press.

References

Parke, R.D., Berkowitz, L., Leyens, J.P., West, S. and Sebastian, R. (1977), The effects of movie violence on juvenile delinquents, IN L. Berkowitz (Ed.), Advances in Experimental Social Psychology, (v.10), New York : Academic Press.

Patterson, G.R. (1979), A Performance Theory for Coercive Family Interaction IN R.B. Cairns, The Analysis of Social Interactions : Methods, Issues and Illustrations, New York: Lawrence Erlbaum Associates.

Piaget, J. (1926), The Language and Thought of the Child, New York : Harcourt, Brace.

Pittman, S.I. (1985), A cognitive ethnography and quantification of a first-grade teacher's selection routines for classroom management, The Elementary School Journal, 85, 4, 541-57.

Polanyi, M. (1964), Personal Knowledge, New York: Harper and Row.

Potter, W. and Slee, P.T. (1986), The Potter-Slee Assessment Check List (P-SAC). Unpublished Report.

Poole, R. (1972), Towards Deep Subjectivity, London : Allen Lane.

Powell, J., Martindale, A. and Kulp, S. (1975), An evaluation of time sampling measures of behaviour, Journal of Applied Behaviour Analysis, 8, 463-9.

Quay, H.C. (1979), Classification IN H.C. Quay and J.S. Werry, Psychological Disorders of Childhood, New York : John Wiley and Sons.

Rapoport, J. and Benoit, M. (1979), The relation of direct home observations to the clinic evaluation of hyperactive school age boys, Journal of Child Psychology and Psychiatry, 16, 141-7.

Reason, P. and Rowan (1981) (Eds), Human Enquiry. A Source Book of New Paradigm Research, Chichester : John Wiley and Sons.

Reed, M. and Edelbrock, C. (1983), Reliability and validity of the direct observation form of the child behaviour checklist, Journal of Abnormal Child Psychology, 11, 521-30.

Richards, M.P.M. and Bernal, J.F. (1971), Social interaction in the first days of life, IN H.R. Schaffer (Ed.), The Origins of Human Social Relations, London : Academic Press.

Richer, J. (1976), The social-avoidance behaviour of autistic children, Animal Behaviour, 24, 898-906.

References

Rist, R. (1977), On the relations among educational research paradigms : From disdain to détente, Anthropology and Education Quarterly, 8, 42-9.

Roberts, M. and Forehand, R. (1978), The assessment of maladaptive parent-child interaction by direct observation : An analysis of methods, Journal of Abnormal Child Psychology, 6, 257-70.

Rosenthal, M.K. (1982), Vocal dialogues in the neonatal period, Developmental Psychology, 18, 17-21.

Royal Commission on Human Relationships (1977), Volume 4, Part V, The Family.

Royce, J. (1964), The Encapsulated Man - An Interdisciplinary Essay on the Search for Meaning, Princeton : Van Nostrand.

Russell, A. (1980), Maternal perceptions of the infant and beliefs about the role of mothers as mediators of child rearing behaviour, Australian Journal of Early Childhood, 5, 19-24.

Russell, A. (1983), Stability of mother-infant interaction from 6 to 12 months, Infant Behaviour and Development, 6, 27-37.

Russell, B. (1974), History of Western Philosophy, London : George Allen and Unwin.

Rutter, M. (1974), A children's behaviour questionnaire for completion by teachers: Preliminary findings, IN P. Williams (Ed.), Behaviour Problems in School, University of London Press.

Rutter, M. Tizard, J. and Whitmore, K. (1970), Education, Health and Behaviour, London : Longman.

Sackett, G.P. (Ed.) (1978), Observing Behaviour, Volume 1. Theory and Applications in Mental Retardation, New York : University Park Press.

Scarlett, W.G. (1979), Social isolation from age mates among nursery school children, Journal of Child Psychology and Psychiatry, 21, 231-40.

Schaffer, H.R., Collis, G.M. and Parsons, G. (1977), Vocal inter-change and visual regard in verbal and pre-verbal children, IN H.R. Schaffer (Ed.), Studies in Mother-Infant Interaction, London : Academic Press.

Schumacher, E.F. (1977), A Guide for the Perplexed, London : Abacus.

References

Schumaker, J., Wildgen, J. and Sherman, J.
(1982), Social interaction of learning
disabled junior high school students in their
regular classrooms : An observational analysis,
Journal of Learning Disabilities, 15, 355-8.

Schwartz, M.S. and Schwartz, C.G. (1955),
Problems in participant observation, American
Journal of Sociology, 60, 343-54.

Shinn, M.W. (1900), The Biography of a Baby : The
First Year of Life, Boston : Houghton-Mifflin.

Simpson, M.J.A. (1979), Problems of recording
behavioural data by keyboard, IN M. Lamb,
S.J. Suomi and G.R. Stephenson (Eds), Social
Interaction Analysis : Methodological Issues,
University of Wisconsin Press.

Slee, P.T. (1982), Mother-infant interaction. The
expression of emotions during the 6-8 month
period of the infant's life, Unpublished
Ph.D. Thesis, Flinders University of South
Australia.

Slee, P.T. (1983,a), Infant emotional development
and parent-child interaction : A contemporary
viewpoint, Australian Journal of Early
Childhood, 8, 33-8.

Slee, P.T. (1983,b), Mother-infant vocal
interaction as a function of emotional
expression, Early Child Development and Care,
11, 33-45.

Slee, P.T. (1984,a), The nature of mother-infant
gaze patterns during interaction as a function
of emotional expression, Journal of the
American Academy of Child Psychiatry, 21,
385-91.

Slee, P.T. (1984,b), Mother-infant interaction:
The stability of emotional expression during
infants' sixth to eighth month, Early Child
Development and Care, 16, 217-31.

Slee, P.T. (1986,a), A study of children's adjustment to kindergarten, Australian Journal of
Early Childhood, 11, 24-7.

Slee, P.T. (1986,b), The relation of temperament
and other factors to children's kindergarten
adjustment, Child Psychiatry and Human
Development, 2, 104-12.

Smith, P. and Connolly, K. (1972), Patterns of
play and social interaction in pre-school
children, IN N.G. Blurton-Jones (Ed.),
Ethological Studies in Child Behaviour,
London : Cambridge University Press.

References

Stanislavski, C. (1948), *An actor prepares*, New York : Theatre Art Books.

Stephenson, G.R. (1979), PLEXYN: A computer-compatible grammar for coding complex social interactions, IN M. Lamb et al., (Eds), *Social Interaction Analysis. Methodological Issues*, The University of Wisconsin Press.

Stern, D.N. (1974), Mother and infant at play: The dyadic interaction involving facial, vocal and gaze behaviours, IN M. Lewis and L.A. Rosenblum (Eds), *The Effect of the Infant on its Care-giver*, New York : John Wiley and Sons.

Stern, D.N. (1977), *The First Relationship: Infant and Mother*, London : Fontana.

Stern, D.N., Jaffe, J., Beebe, B. and Bennett, S.L. (1975), Vocalising in unison and in alternation : Two modes of communication within the mother-infant dyad, *Annals of New York Academy of Sciences*, 163, 89-100.

Strauss, A., Schatzman, L., Bucher, R., Ehrlich, D., and Sabshin, M. (1964), *Psychiatric Ideologies and Institutions*, New York : Free Press.

Strupp, H.H. and Hadley, S.W. (1977), A tripartite model of mental health and therapeutic outcomes, *American Psychologist*, 32, 2, 187-96.

Sturge, C. (1982), Reading retardation and antisocial behaviour, *Journal of Child Psychology and Psychiatry*, 23, 21-31.

Thomas, A., Chess, S. and Birch, H. (1969), *Temperament and Behaviour Disorders in Children*, New York : University Press.

Thompson, F. (1947), *The Hound of Heaven*, London: A.R. Mowbray and Company Limited.

Thoreau, D. (1960), *Walden and Civil Disobedience*, New York : A Signet Classic.

Tiedemann, D. (1787), *Beobach Tungen Ueber Die Entwickelung Des Seelenfahrigkeiten Bel Kindern*, Altenburg : Bonde.

Tizard, J. (1974), Questionnaire measures of maladjustment, IN P. Williams, *Behaviour Problems in School*, University of London Press.

Tomkins, S. (1966), Affect and the psychology of knowledge, IN S. Tomkins and C. Izard (Eds), *Affect, Cognition and Personality : Empirical Studies*, New York : Springer.

Toulmin, S. (1972), *Human Understanding*, Princeton : University Press.

References

Twentyman, C.T. and Martin, B. (1978), Modification of problem interaction in mother-child dyads by modeling and behaviour rehearsal, Journal of Clinical Psychology, 34, 138-43.

Van Leeuwen, M.S. (1982), Reflexivity in North American Psychology : Historical reflections on one aspect of a changing paradigm. Unpublished Paper. Department of Psychology, York University.

Vidich, A.J. (1955), Participant observation and the collection and interpretation of data, American Journal of Sociology, 60, 354-60.

Viney, L. (1985), Editorial, Australian Psychologist, 20, 1-2.

Waters, E. (1978), The reliability and stability of individual differences in infant-mother attachment, Child Development, 49, 483-94.

Watts, R. (1978), Epistemological totalitarianism: the positivist theme in social welfare research, S.A.A.N.Z. Unpublished Paper.

Weil, S. (1973), Waiting on God, London : Collins Fontana Books.

Whyte, W.F. (1955), Street Corner Society, Chicago : University of Chicago Press.

Whyte, W.F. (1960), Interviewing in field research, IN R.N. Adams and J.J. Preiss (Eds), Human Organisation Research, Homewood, Illinois : Dorsey Press.

Wildman, R. and Simon, S.J. (1978), An indirect method for increasing the rate of social interaction in an autistic child, Journal of Clinical Psychology, 34, 144-9.

Wimberger, H.C. and Kogan, K.L. (1968), Interpersonal behaviour ratings, The Journal of Nervous and Mental Disease, 147, 260-71.

Wright, H.F. (1956), Psychological development in midwest, Child Development, 27, 265-86.

Wright, H.F. (1960), Observational child study, IN P.H. Mussen (Ed.), Handbook of Research Methods in Child Development, New York : Wiley.

Wright, H.F. (1967), Recording and Analysing Child Behaviour, New York : Harper and Row.

Yarrow, L.J. and Anderson, B.J. (1979), Procedures for studying parent-infant interaction : A critique, IN E.B. Thoman (Ed.), Origins of the Infant's Social Responsiveness, New York: John Wiley and Sons.

Yarrow, L.J., Rubenstein, J.L. and Pedersen, F.A. (1975), Infant and Environment : Early Cognitive and Motivational Development, New York : Hulsted.

References

Yarrow, M.R. and Waxler, C.Z. (1979), Observing interaction : A confrontation with methodology, IN R.B. Cairns (Ed.), The Analysis of Social Interactions : Methods Issues and Illustrations, New York : John Wiley and Sons.

Young, R. (1981), A study of teacher epistemologies, The Australian Journal of Education, 25, 194-208.

Zegiob, L.E. and Forehand, R. (1975), Maternal interactive behaviour as a function of rare socioeconomic status and sex of the child, Child Development, 46, 564-8.

Zucker, R.A., Manosevitz, M. and Lanyon, R. (1968), Birth order, anxiety and affiliation during crisis, Journal of Personality and Social Psychology, 8, 354-9.

Zukav, G. (1979), The Dancing Wu Li Masters, New York : Fontana.

agency: The idea that a person has the
                   ability to initiate, direct, man-
                   age and control his or her behav-
                   iour.
ecological: An approach to psychology which
                   asserts that the individual is
                   more than the summation of social
                   behaviour, motivation, emotion
                   and so on. It is also the way an
                   individual relates to the envir-
                   onment.
empiricism: The philosophy that sense experi-
                   ence is the only reliable source
                   of knowledge.
epistemology: The knowledge base of any discip-
                   line.
ex post facto: After the fact.
hermeneutic: The science of interpretation.
                   Originally referred to interpret-
                   ing the Scriptures.
hypotheses: A supposition about the relation
                   between two or more variables.
operationalise: To assign meaning to a construct
                   by identifying the activities or
                   'operations' necessary to measure
                   it.
paradigm: A pattern, model, example or world
                   view.
positivism: In general terms positivism
                   refers to a branch of thought in
                   philosophy which attempted to use
                   the methods and principles of the
                   natural sciences in the study of
                   human behaviour.

Glossary of Terms

reflexivity: The capacity for self reflection in human behaviour. The ability to reflect upon the meaning of behaviour - attribute meaning and intention.

reliability: Refers to the dependability, stability, predictability in the measurement of a set of objects.

scientism: The notion that empirical science is the sole arbiter of knowledge.

theory: Sets of interconnected conventions, definitions or propositions proposed to provide, explain or predict a particular phenomenon.

variable: A symbol to which values are assigned. It can be multi-dimensional. Some variables have either-or qualities, e.g., male-female while other variables have a continuous nature, e.g., intelligence.

APPENDIX

INTRODUCTION
In reviewing contemporary child development journals it is possible to identify a range of observation schemes used for child study. The six observation schemes described here demonstrate the:
- range of application of child observation,
- different methods for recording and analysing data
- range of behaviours chosen for observation.

EYBERG, S. and ROBINSON, E., DYADIC PARENT-CHILD INTERACTION CODING SYSTEM (DPICS)

Purpose.
  The DPICS provides the means for assessing the quality of social interaction between parents and children (children aged 2-10 years). It can be used in the study of normal and behaviour problem children.
Setting and Equipment.
  The scheme is suitable for use in both clinic and natural home settings and requires no special equipment.
Coding Scheme.
  As developed the DPICS incorporates 29 separate behaviours that are coded every time they occur for a 5 minute segment, for a total of 3 segments including (i) child directed play, (ii) parent directed play and (iii) clean up. Parent behaviour includes: descriptive statement, reflective statement, descriptive/reflective question, acknowledgement, physical positive, physical negative, labelled praise, unlabelled praise, critical statement, direct command, indirect command. Each command is coded as to whether the child complies, noncomplies or is given no chance to comply.

Child behaviours include: whine, cry, yell, smart talk, physical negative, destructive and changes activity. Note is made of whether the parent responds to or ignores each deviant behaviour.

Reliability and Validity.
Research (Robinson & Eyberg, 1981) has shown the DPICS to have reliability coefficients of 0.91 for adult behaviours and 0.92 for child behaviours. In the same study the scheme correctly classified 100% of normal and 85% of clinic referred families and the procedure predicted 61% of the variance in home behaviour problems.

REFERENCES

Robinson, E., Eyberg, S. (1981), The dyadic parent-child interaction coding system: standardisation and validation, Journal of Consulting and Clinical Psychology, 49, 245-50.
Webster-Stratton, C. (1985), Comparisons of behaviour transactions between conduct-disordered children and their mothers in the clinic and at home, Journal of Abnormal Child Psychology, 13, 169-84.

DODGE, K.A., CODING SYSTEM FOR PEER ORIENTED BEHAVIOUR.

Purpose.
This coding scheme was developed to classify children's behaviour which leads to aggression and social rejection.
It has been used with children aged 7-8 years.
Setting and Equipment.
The scheme has been used in play room settings and requires no special equipment.
Coding Scheme.
The event coding scheme involves coding the context: solitary, interactive, on-task, off-task.
Behaviours are coded into five types incorporating 18 behaviours: (i) solitary activity, (ii) interactive play, (iii) verbalisation, (iv) physical contact with peers, (v) interaction with group leader.
In addition the peer target of each behaviour is noted as is the peer's reaction to the behaviour.

Appendix

Reliability.
Reliability coefficients are 0.96 for contact and 0.77 for the behaviours scored.

REFERENCES

Dodge, K.A. (1983), Behaviour antecedents of peer social status, Child Development, 54, 1386-99.

GAENSBAUER, T. and Mrazek, D., AFFECTIVE EXPRESSION IN INFANTS.

Purpose.
The focus of this scheme is the assessment of infant emotional expression. More particularly, it is designed to assess infant emotional expression in a series of structured interactions involving the child's mother and a stranger. The five observational phases are: (i) a 7 minute play period between mother and infant, (ii) a 5 minute stranger-approach period, (iii) a 15-25 minute period for administering the Bayley developmental test, (iv) a 3 minute mother-separation and 2 minute reunion, and (v) a 3 minute period of mother-infant play following stranger departure. The scheme has been used in the study of normal and abused infants.
Setting and Equipment.
Laboratory setting. The session is video-taped.
Coding Scheme.
The six infant emotions of pleasure, interest, fear, anger, sadness and distress are rated on a nine point scale at 30 second intervals.
Reliability.
Reliability coefficients are in the range 0.60 to 0.80.

REFERENCES

Gaensbauer, T., Mrazek, D. and Emde, R. (1979), Patterning of emotional response in a playroom laboratory situation, Infant Behaviour and Development, 2, 163-78.
Gaensbauer, T. and Mrazek, D. (1981), Affective expression in infants, Journal of the American Academy of Child Psychiatry, 20, 673-91.

Appendix

SLEE, P.T., THE FLINDERS MOTHER-INFANT CODING
SCHEME (FM-ICS).

Purpose.
The FM-ICS was developed for the purpose of
assessing a range of behaviour between mothers
and infants. The scheme is designed to
facilitate analysis of sequences of vocal and
gaze behaviour. It also combines coding of
discrete behaviour categories and ratings of
infants' and mothers' emotional expressions.
Settings and Equipment.
The scheme is designed to be used in the
natural home setting and requires video-taping
of unstructured mother-infant interactions
which are subsequently coded.
Coding Scheme.
Behaviours coded for both mother and infant
include: (i) interactive state, (ii) context,
(iii) proximity, (iv) activity, (v) facial
expression, (vi), vocalization, (vii) gaze.
In addition mothers and infants are rated for
emotional expression using the emotions
affection, warm, neutral, cold and hostile.
A continuous time sampling procedure is used
with each five second interval being scored
for the behaviours listed.
Reliability.
Reliability coefficients average 0.82 for all
categories.

REFERENCES

Slee, P.T. (1982), Mother-infant interaction : The
expression of emotions during the 6-8 month
period of the infant's life. Unpublished
Ph.D. Thesis.
Slee, P.T. (1984), The nature of mother-infant
gaze patterns during interaction as a function
of emotional expression, Journal of the
American Academy of Child Psychiatry, 21,
385-91.

REED, M. and EDELBROCK, C., THE DIRECT OBSERVATION
FORM (DOF).

Purpose.
This observation scheme developed from the
Child Behaviour Checklist was developed to
help identify children experiencing emotional
and or behavioural disorders. It was also

157

Appendix

considered to have application in making clinical and educational decisions regarding disturbed children and for evaluating change in behaviour over time.

Setting and Equipment.

The DOF was designed for use in classroom settings and requires no sophisticated data collection equipment or lengthy observer training. It could be used with children ranging in age from 6-11.

Coding Scheme.

The scheme comprises 96 behaviour problem items and a measure of on-task behaviour. The procedure involves observing a child for 10 minutes and writing a narrative account of his/her behaviour. Each of the 96 items is then rated on 0-1-2-3 response scale where 0 indicates the behaviour was not observed, 1 indicates a slight occurrence, 2 a definite occurrence with mild intensity and 3 indicated an occurrence with severe intensity. A total behaviour problem score is derived from the sum of the 96 items. The DOF also provides a measure of on-task behaviour scored during the last five seconds of each minute of observation. The child receives 1 point if his/her behaviour is on-task and 0 if it is not.

Reliability and Validity.

Inter-observer reliability is 0.91 for the total score and 0.71 for on-task scores. For the 96 behaviours the majority of items have a reliability exceeding 0.80. The DOF offers some discriminant validity with disturbed boys obtaining significantly higher total problem scores and lower on-task scores than normal boys.

REFERENCES

Reed, M. and Edelbrock, C. (1983), Reliability and validity of the Direct Observation Form of the child behaviour checklist, Journal of Abnormal Child Psychology, 11, 4, 521-30.

FREEMAN, B., RITVO, E., GUTHRIE, D., SCHROTH, P. and BALL, J. THE BEHAVIOUR OBSERVATION SCALE FOR AUTISM (BOS).

Purpose.

The BOS was developed to compare behaviours of

Appendix

autistic children with behaviours of normal and mentally retarded children. In developing the scale every effort was made to ensure that behaviours coded were (i) independent of a theoretical model or bias, (ii) objectively defined, (iii) reliably scorable and (iv) suitable for statistical analysis.

Setting and Equipment.
The scale was designed for use in a laboratory setting and requires little in the way of elaborate equipment.

Coding Scheme.
The scale consists of 67 behaviours in a checklist form. In a free play situation the behaviours are recorded in 9 three minute intervals. Behaviours are scored as not present, occurring once or twice or occurring continuously during a three minute interval. Apart from 1 three minute interval where the examiner attempts to engage in a ball game, she/he remains seated in one corner of the examination room.

Reliability and Validity.
Reliability coefficients greater than 0.84 have been recorded for all but 12 of the 67 behaviours. The instrument does discriminate between normal and autistic and handicapped children's behaviour.

REFERENCES

Freeman, B., Ritvo, E., Guthrie, D., Schroth, P. and Ball, J. (1978), The Behaviour Observation Scale for Autism, Journal of the American Academy of Child Psychiatry, 17, 570-88.

Subject Index

Name Index

163

Name Index

Name Index